CULTIVATING
THE COOK'S
GARDEN

Cultivating the Cook's Garden

THEODORE JAMES, JR.

COUNCIL OAK BOOKS

TULSA AND SAN FRANCISCO

COUNCIL OAK BOOKS

TULSA, OKLAHOMA 74120

1.800.247.8850

COPYRIGHT ©1983 AND 1998 BY THEODORE JAMES, JR.

FIRST EDITION PUBLISHED AS *The Gourmet Garden* IN 1983

BY E.P. DUTTON, INC.

ALL RIGHTS RESERVED.

05 04 03 02 01 00 99 98 5 4 3 2 1

ISBN 1-57178-065-3

DESIGNED AND EDITED BY CAROL HARALSON

LIBRARY OF CONGRESS CATALOGING-IN-PUBLICATION DATA

JAMES, THEODORE.

THE COOK'S GARDEN : DELICIOUSLY FRESH THINGS TO EAT,

JUST OUTSIDE YOUR KITCHEN DOOR / THEODORE JAMES, JR.

P.   CM.

REV. ED. OF: THE GOURMET GARDEN. 1ST ED. C1983.

INCLUDES INDEX.

ISBN 1-57178-065-3 (PBK.)

1. VEGETABLE GARDENING. 2. FRUIT-CULTURE. 3. HERB

GARDENING. 4. ORGANIC GARDENING. 5. COOKERY

(VEGETABLES) 6. COOKERY (FRUIT) 7. COOKERY (HERBS) 8.

KITCHEN GARDENS. I. JAMES, THEODORE. GOURMET GARDEN.

II. TITLE.

SB324.3.J35 1998

635–DC21   98-11487

CIP

THE GOOD GARDENER COMMONLY BORROWS
HIS METHODS, IF NOT HIS GOALS, FROM
NATURE HERSELF. FOR THOUGH NATURE
DOESN'T SEEM TO DICTATE IN ADVANCE WHAT
WE CAN DO IN A PLACE—WE ARE FREE, IN THE
SAME WAY EVOLUTION IS, TO TRY SOMETHING
COMPLETELY NEW—IN THE END SHE WILL LET
US KNOW WHAT DOES AND DOES NOT WORK.
SHE IS ABOVE ALL A PRAGMATIST, AND SO IS
THE SUCCESSFUL GARDENER.

Michael Pollan, *Second Nature*

DOES A GARDEN PAY? AS I LOOK AT IT, YOU

MIGHT AS WELL ASK, DOES A SUNSET PAY?

Charles Dudley Warner, *My Summer in a Garden*

CONTENTS

Vegetables

Herbs

Berries

SOURCES

INDEX

THE FIRST EDITION OF THIS BOOK was published in 1983. Not surprisingly, many changes were made in preparing the present completely updated and revised edition. But the amazing thing to me is how these revisions reflect the changes in America's eating habits. Vegetables that few people knew about 15 years ago—daikon, radicchio, broccoli raab, tomatillos, jalapeños, arugula—are now standard in many gardens. Increasing interest in far-flung cuisines created a demand for these vegetables by cooks and gardeners, and it was met by suppliers, scientists, and hybridizers with scores of new and exciting varieties of vegetables and herbs. Now they are grown everywhere, and are even available in many supermarkets. With the infusion of Tex-Mex, California, Japanese, Vietnamese, Cajun, and Thai cuisines into mainstream American cooking has come a demand for the particular vegetables and herbs essential to their creation. And, if they are not readily available in the markets, enterprising gardeners and cooks have taken to growing them at home, in their own gardens.

Fifteen years ago, international cuisines were usually sampled abroad and then recreated at home by those Americans who could afford extensive travel. But today, travel is not necessarily the initial exposure to these once rarified foods. Restaurants all over the country offer East Indian tandoori specialties, Indonesian coconut-milk curries, aromatic Thai soups, Japanese stir-fries, couscous, paella, tamales, sushi. Cookbooks and cooking magazines counsel the enterprising and the intrepid on how to make these dishes at home.

Consider that these treats are grown by average people in their countries of origin. So, you will find that there is nothing "tricky" about growing them.

To begin with, I assume that if you are interested in growing specialty vegetables and herbs, you have had a bit of gardening experience, or at least know where to obtain guidance in the basics. In other words, you know what rototilling is, you know how to cultivate with a hoe, you are aware that compost is like gold. And you know that if it doesn't rain for a week it's time to drag out the hose and sprinkle. And that light requirements for most plants are somewhat flexible. That is, if full sun is recommended for a particular plant, often that plant will thrive in partial shade.

And rather than discussing planting, cultivation, watering, pruning, harvesting, pest and disease control, mulching, fertilizing, and other aspects of gardening in separate chapters of this book, all instructions pertaining to each vegetable, herb, or berry are included in each individual entry. I think you'll find this a far more convenient way to learn about growing varieties you opt to plant rather than having to thumb through cross-references and appendixes.

You will notice as you read through this book that many "Gardener's Tips" are included at the end of each entry. Do not ignore them. They include advice garnered from many experienced sources through the years, as well as my own comments. They will help you to succeed with your garden.

I have also included cooking tips—suggestions or recipes concerned with the preparation of your crops for eating and preserving. While I hope these tips may give pleasure or spark a new culinary idea, they are not intended to be the last word on preparing the succulent bounty of your garden. Consult your favorite cookbooks for further suggestions.

Before moving on, you might wish to consider growing your produce in the organic manner. Experience has shown that crops grown organically taste better and are more healthful not only for you but for the environment as well. For this reason, right at the start, I include a formula for an organic fertilizer which you may choose to use rather than the chemically produced 5-10-5.

This recipe for organic fertilizer was entrusted to me by a flamboyant Hungarian gardener friend, long since gone. Behind his colorful demeanor, he was a scientist and had spent years developing the following formula for organic enriching material. Here it is:

In an eight-gallon container, such as a rubber trash can, prepare your fertilizer mix. The proportion should be roughly 30 percent dried sheep or cow manure (horse manure is not recommended until it has been thoroughly composted for one year), 20 percent good compost or peat moss, 10 percent bloodmeal, 10 percent bonemeal, 15 percent superphosphate or natural rock phosphate, 10 percent ground limestone, and 5 percent vermiculite. Use this instead of 5-10-5 fertilizer, roughly doubling the amount specified for each application.

In keeping with the trend toward organic solutions, you can also use nontoxic or organic substances to control many pests and diseases. I will stress this aspect of control throughout the book whenever practical. As a rule of thumb, when you plan your garden, interplant among your crops the following: old-fashioned French marigolds, nasturtiums, herbs of all varieties, and garlic—lots of it. They all help to ward off pests and disease.

One final bit of preliminary advice for general gardening of all kinds. Put up a fence! And make that fence high enough (four feet is minimum) and dense enough to ward off rabbits, stray dogs, and other animals. The investment is quite small compared to the damage that several rabbits or dogs can wreak in a season or two, let alone overnight. Your fence will also serve as a trellis for peas, beans, tomatoes, cucumbers, and melons, conserving space and saving trouble in fashioning supports for individual crops.

If deer are visitors in your area, make your fence eight feet tall, and if woodchucks, gophers, or other burrowing creatures are your neighbors, bury your fence one foot deep.

A postscript: Remember your friends—the insects, birds, and reptiles that will help you in your pursuit of growing fine produce. If you are a gardener, you likely feed the birds during winter. Continue to do so in the summer. Oh, yes, there are some delectables that they enjoy, but birds will repay you ten times over for the meals they may take from your garden by eating hundreds of thousands of undesirable insects. Do not kill toads or garter snakes; they consume their weight in pests every week. Learn which insects are beneficial to your garden. Among them are ladybugs, praying mantises, ground beetles, the iridescent blue-green European ground beetle, and the tiger beetle. Also the robber fly, assassin bug, goldeneyed lacewing, ant-lion (also called doodlebug), damsel bug, syrphid fly (also called flower fly), and the wasp. They attack and kill many pests that rob you of food.

Also cherish the pollinating insects such as bees. Without them, we would certainly all be very hungry.

So, if you can't resist the temptation to treat yourself to the best that nature has to offer, read on, for this book will teach you much of what you must know to enjoy the remarkable bounty of a garden filled with wonderful vegetables, berries, and herbs.

Here is what you'll find in each entry:

THE PLANT'S COMMON NAME — THE ONE YOU'LL FIND MOST OFTEN ON SEED PACKETS AND IN COOKBOOKS.

THE PLANT'S SCIENTIFIC NAME — FIRST ITS GENUS AND THEN ITS SPECIES. THIS IS SOMETHING LIKE THE PLANT'S SURNAME AND GIVEN NAME. KNOWING A PLANT'S SCIENTIFIC NAME IS USEFUL TO AN UNDERSTANDING OF HOW PLANTS ARE RELATED IN FAMILIES THAT SHARE PARTICULAR TRAITS.

WHEN SPECIES SHOW MINOR VARIATIONS IN CHARACTER, THEY ARE GIVEN A THIRD NAME, CALLED A VARIETY NAME. A CULTIVAR, OR CULTIVATED VARIETY, IS ONE THAT HAS BEEN SELECTED FROM THE WILD OR FROM GARDENS AND GROWN IN CULTIVATION. THE CHARACTERISTICS OF SUCH A PLANT ARE PROTECTED BY CONTROLLED PROPAGATION.

VEGETABLES   8 7

PEAS

(Pisum sativum)

Petits Pois are the tiny little beebee peas favored by the French. Cultivation is easy. The secret is knowing when to harvest.

HARDINESS: Annual, tender.

WHEN TO PLANT: In early spring, when ground is workable.

SPACING: Double rows 1 foot apart. Allow 2 feet between every three rows for better ventilation. Plant fifteen seeds per foot.

DEPTH: 1 inch.

HARVEST TIME: 6 to 7 weeks.

HOW TO GROW PETITS POIS: Peas are an early crop, suffering in the heat and drought of summer, so you must plant them early—late March to early April. Work in compost, rotted manure, and 5-10-5 fertilizer or organic mixture. Plant seeds fifteen per foot.

GARDENER'S TIP 3

Inoculate your peas before planting. Purchase legume inoculant from a garden center, moisten the seed, pour on the powder, roll the seed in the powder, coating it generously, and plant the seed. Your germination success and yield will be greater.

PESTS: Pea weevils are brown with gray, black, and white markings and are 1/5 inch long. They damage blossoms and lay egg clusters on young pods. To control use a 57 percent Malathion EC solution (2 tablespoons to 1 gallon of water) and spray while they blossom and before the first pods form. Stop spraying 7 days before harvest.

VARIETIES: Petit Provencal is early and very productive. A new variety, Fabina, is a gourmet treat as well. Both freeze well.

COOKING TIP 1

Steam the peas for several minutes, till tender but still slightly crunchy, and serve with melted butter. As with most Epicurean vegetables, they are at their best served plain with butter.

HARDINESS: THIS ITEM TELLS YOU ABOUT THE PLANT'S LIFESPAN AND ABILITY TO WITHSTAND CLIMACTIC EXTREMITIES.

ANNUALS ARE PLANTS THAT COMPLETE THEIR LIFE CYCLE — GERMINATING, FLOWERING, SEEDING, AND DYING — IN ONE GROWING SEASON. A PERENNIAL IS A PLANT THAT LIVES FOR AT LEAST THREE SEASONS; MANY MAY LIVE FOR DECADES.

A HARDY PLANT IS ONE THAT CAN WITHSTAND YEAR-ROUND WEATHER CONDITIONS.

TENDER PLANTS ARE THOSE USUALLY UNABLE TO WITHSTAND TEMPERATURES BELOW 20° F.

HARDINESS ZONES ARE BASED ON THE AVERAGE LOWEST TEMPERATURES THAT CAN BE EXPECTED IN A GIVEN AREA. IN GENERAL, THESE ARE THE TEMPERATURE ZONES OF THE US:

ZONE 1	BELOW 50° F.
ZONE 2	-50° TO -40° F.
ZONE 3	-40° TO -30° F.
ZONE 4	-30° TO -20° F.
ZONE 5	-20° TO -10° F.
ZONE 6	-10° TO 0° F.
ZONE 7	0° TO 10° F.
ZONE 8	10° TO 20° F.
ZONE 9	20° TO 30° F.
ZONE 10	30° TO 40° F.
ZONE 11	ABOVE 40° F.

WHEN AND HOW TO PLANT, AND WHEN TO HARVEST YOUR CROP.

GARDENER'S TIPS — BITS OF WISDOM SPECIFIC TO A GIVEN PLANT THAT WILL HELP YOU MAKE THE MOST OF IT IN YOUR GARDEN.

PESTS — WHO MAY BE AFTER YOUR VEGETABLE OR HERB AND HOW TO HEAD THEM OFF AT THE PASS.

COOKING TIPS — RECIPES, SUGGESTIONS, AND IDEAS FOR TAKING THE MAXIMUM PLEASURE FROM YOUR CROPS ONCE YOU GET THEM TO THE KITCHEN.

SPECIAL "HOW-TO-GROW" INFORMATION ABOUT THE PLANT'S PREFERENCES AND IDIOSYNCRASIES, AND HOW TO MAKE IT FEEL AT HOME IN YOUR GARDEN.

VEGETABLES

WHEN YOU PLANT annual vegetable and herb seeds, you can either sow them directly in the garden at the recommended time during the growing season or you can install a simple, inexpensive lighting system and start seeds under lights. There are many advantages to this system. Keep in mind that some seeds should be sprinkled on the soil surface and kept evenly moist at all times because they require light to germinate. Others should be planted and covered with soil because they require dark conditions to germinate. All seed packages include this information. If you wish to start seeds under lights indoors, you will get a head start on your garden, and have better control over moisture and light requirements. Here's how to install a simple lighting arrangement for your seeds, and at about 1/4 the price of one which you may find in your garden center.

Purchase a four-foot long industrial fluorescent light fixture. They cost about $15 in most home improvement centers. Fixtures usually come with lights, both cool tubes. Substitute one warm tube for one of the cool tubes. There is no need to buy expensive, special plant growing fluorescent tubes. Despite manufacturer's claims, results for starting seedlings are just about equally as good with one cool and one hot tube. Either hang the fixture in a heated basement over a table or work bench, or attach it to the bottom of a shelf in the house. Plug it in and you are ready to start seeds indoors at the proper time.

Since fixtures should remain on for about 14 hours a day, you may want to buy a timer switch to turn lights off and on if you don't wish to be bothered with this daily task. These cost less than $10. You can start with one fixture, however even at the beginning, you will find that you will want at least two. And after several years, you will undoubtedly find that you will want three or four to accommodate the plants you wish to start from seed.

You can sow seeds in just about any container imaginable: milk cartons, plastic containers, flower pots, aluminum trays, in short anything that will hold a seed-starting soil mixture. Be advised that drainage must be provided, so if you use homemade containers, poke holes through the bottoms so that excess water can escape. You will have reasonable success using these containers. Beyond the home made, there are many products available in garden centers and nurseries which are made specifically for starting seeds.

Every now and then, however, something comes on the market which is so exceptional, so easy to use, and which results in such total success that it is worth investigating. If you wish to start seeds indoors under lights, it will be well worth your time to write to: Gardener's Supply Co., 128 Intervale Road, Burlington, VT 05401, (802) 863-4535. They import from England seed-starting kits called A. P. Propatop, which are made of styrofoam and include a reservoir arrangement and felt which by a process similar to wick watering maintains even moisture for the seed trays. This cuts down tremendously on the watering process. Trays hold about three to four quarts of water, and once filled can be checked perhaps once a week to see if they need refilling.

Seedlings are watered from the bottom, so they are not damaged by the force of top watering. A clear plastic top is included to create a mini-greenhouse assuring that humidity is maintained.

These units are a Godsend to the busy gardener. They are very reasonable in price, can be reused again and again during the season as well as year in and year out, and are also useful for rooting cuttings, watering house plants when you are away from home, in short, absolutely indispensable to the home gardener. A four foot industrial fluorescent light fixture will accommodate three of these self watering seed starter trays. Although you will have to invest some money in setting up an indoor light system, consider that a package of six annual plants costs around $3 these days. Each of the A. P. Propatop units contains 40 spaces for growing plants. If you start with three, you can grow 120 plants. These same plants would cost you around $60 at nurseries and garden centers. Quite a substantial savings indeed. In addition, you will have the pleasure of watching seedlings grow during the late winter, early spring months.

So then, whether you use makeshift containers or avail yourself of the above units, the only other thing you will need to start seeds indoors is the proper soil. Do not purchase potting soil, as it is too heavy in texture to start seeds. Terra-lite or Reddi-Mix, available in garden centers and nurseries are two products mixed to provide perfect growing conditions for starting seeds. They are sterilized, include vermiculite to lighten soil and retain moisture and are recommended. Before placing these products in a container, moisten them thoroughly. Then plant seeds according to instructions on packet, that is either lightly covered with soil or on soil surface. If you are using a seed-starting unit which you purchased, plant several seeds in each individual compartment. Insert labels in proper places. Place under lights for 14 hours a day with soil surface about two inches from light tube surface. If you are using a homemade container, mist with room temperature water, using a mister available in garden centers and nurseries, until soil is evenly moist.

If you use the A. P. Propatop unit or a similar setup, the reservoir will provide the proper amount of water. When seedlings are about one-half inch high, using cuticle scissors, cut off all but the strongest in each compartment. Once a week, feed with all-purpose liquid house plant fertilizer at one-quarter strength recommended by manufacturer. About one week before outdoor planting time you must harden off your plants. This date varies from location to location throughout the country, however if plants are to be set out after "all danger of frost," check locally to find out when it is safe to plant tomatoes outdoors. Planting time for these annuals will be the same. This will acclimate them to the strong sunlight and cool nights of outdoor growing. You do this by placing containers outdoors in a shady spot during the day and bringing them indoors at night. Two days later, place them in a sunny spot for about half a day and a shady spot for the other half, then the next day leave them in the sun for the entire day and bring them indoors only if the night is to be chilly. In any event, if it rains bring them indoors. If plants' leaves start to look bleached, they are receiving too much sun and are not yet accustomed to the strong light. Move them back into shade. After about one week, you can safely plant them in your garden where you want them.

ARTICHOKES

(Cynara Scolymus, Globe Artichoke)

Members of the thistle family, these delectable, somewhat bizarre vegetables—actually the large flower buds of the plant—are a treat. But be sure not to eat the thorns. You won't like them. Artichokes are rarely grown in this country except in the very warm areas of California, but they can and will thrive in many less ideal conditions.

HARDINESS: Perennial in warm climates (Zones 8-10), can be grown as an annual in any area with a minimum of 100 frost-free days. Otherwise, buy vegetables in the supermarket, because your climate is too cold for them.

WHEN TO PLANT: Start seeds indoors the same time you start tomatoes, about 8-10 weeks before all danger of frost outdoors. You may also buy plants ready to set out from a reputable nursery. If you choose to start from seed, refrigerate seeds for two weeks before planting them. This helps break dormancy and assures better germination. Plant outdoors after all danger of frost.

SPACING: When seedlings are about 8-10 inches high, set 3 feet apart.

DEPTH: Plant at same soil level as grown indoors or as exists in purchased nursery pots.

HARVEST TIME: Late summer to early fall, when buds are the size of your fist, but before the purple petals of the flower are visible. Smaller is better in this case. Large artichokes can be tough.

HOW TO GROW ARTICHOKES: Select a site in full sun. Before planting, improve soil substantially. Artichokes are very heavy feeders so add about 50 percent garden compost, well rotted manure or leaf mold to the soil. Also add 5-10-5 fertilizer in amounts on package label. Once planted, water copiously, since they require almost constantly moist soil.

Gardener's Tip 1

If you live in a moderately cool climate (Zones 6-7), you might consider overwintering your plants bare root in a cool, dark place in the basement, and then replanting them in the spring after frost period.

PESTS: Aphids may strike. They mass in groups along tips of new shoots and attack buds. Dislodge them with jets of water from a garden hose. You can also rub them off with your fingers as they gather. Slugs and snails may attach when the plants are young. The age-old solution for these is to place a shallow pie plate filled with beer near the plant. Born boozers, slugs make their way to the beer, climb in and drown in the suds.

VARIETIES: Grande Beurre (160 days from sowing to harvest), Green Globe (180 days from sowing to harvest).

Cooking Tip 1

It's easy to cook an artichoke. Cut off the stem, leaving about one inch of it below the bottom of the bud. Tear or cut off the tough outer leaves at the bottom of the bud. With a sharp knife, cut off about one inch of the pointed top of the bud, straight across. Wash the bud, then put it into a pot along with salt, some lemon juice, and water to cover. Simmer for 30-45 minutes and fork test for tenderness. Remove from water and drain water from bud.

You can simply dip leaf after leaf in melted butter, and scrape off the flesh from the inner side of each leaf with your teeth. Offer diners an extra plate on which to discard the scraped leaves. Or, warm a little mayonnaise, add lemon juice to taste, and enjoy the leaves dipped in that mixture.

ARUGULA

Arugula selvatica

The peppery tang of arugula (also called roquette or rocket) is ubiquitous on the tables of elegant northern Italian restaurants, or for that matter on *al fresco* tables of Italian peasants in the same district. Occasionally this vegetable is available in ethnic markets at reasonable prices, or in pricey food emporiums exorbitantly. Grow it yourself. It is virtually disease- and pest-free, foolproof to cultivate, and a delight to the palate. Considering that a package of seeds will cost you about one dollar, as compared to a five-dollar salad at a trendy restaurant, and further considering that your package of seeds, with a minimum of care, will probably produce enough salads to turn the Italian navy green, well . . . enough said.

HARDINESS: Annual, very hardy.

WHEN TO PLANT: In early spring, as soon as ground is workable, then successively every 10 days throughout the season.

SPACING: Rows about 1 foot apart; plant seeds thinly.

DEPTH: 1/4 inch.

HARVEST TIME: From 3 to 5 weeks. Arugula will go to seed after about 6 weeks.

HOW TO GROW ARUGULA: Plant in full sun as soon as ground is workable and then every 10 days for a continuous supply of young leaves. Sow tiny seeds rather thinly about 1/4 inch deep. You would do well to mix the seeds with sand before sowing in order to ensure a thinly sowed crop. Cover with soil and keep well watered until seeds germinate. You should be able to pick some of your crop in about 4 weeks to add zest to salads. After that, you can pick young leaves and make a salad using only arugula. This plant goes to seed in about 6 weeks, so plan on successive plantings.

GARDENER'S TIP 1

As the plants bolt, pull them out of the soil. Quality deteriorates as the plant ages. However, if you plant successive crops, you should not have to be without plenty of this delicious salad ingredient all through the season.

GARDENER'S TIP 2

As the season draws to a close, be sure to allow some of your plants to go to seed. Collect the seeds, and store over the winter in airtight containers in a cool, dark place. The back of the refrigerator will do. Once in the refrigerator, be sure not to confuse your arugula seeds with leftovers and throw them out. In most parts of the country, arugula will not self sow for an early spring crop.

PESTS: There are none.

VARIETIES: Simply arugula, rocket or roquette.

COOKING TIP 1

If you have not yet acquired a taste for arugula, try some mixed with romaine, Boston, or leaf lettuce in a salad. You'll find that before long, you'll crave more, ultimately finding a pure arugula salad to your liking. It is also delectable when combined with sliced beefsteak tomatoes in a vinaigrette dressing.

COOKING TIP 2

As arugula ages, the leaves become somewhat tough and are really no longer desirable for salads. However, at that state of their maturity, they are excellent in soups. Consult any basic Chinese cookbook for an egg drop soup recipe. Then, instead of adding bok choy to the soup, add a reasonable amount of arugula to it. Coarsely chopped leaves are also delicious in cream soups such as cream of carrot, celery, onion or chicken, or in creamy cheese soups. Add them when the soup is very nearly finished so they retain some body. The cream will abate the natural bite of the green so that even people who have yet to acquire a taste for arugula often enjoy it in a velvety cream soup.

ASPARAGUS

(Asparagus officinalis)

In Europe, almost all asparagus is blanched; consequently it is a very pale yellow-green color when in the markets, as compared to our deep green, purple-tipped specimens. I traveled to the heart of the Belgian asparagus country to see firsthand just how the blanching process is accomplished. Instructions are included below. Keep in mind that blanched asparagus has a different taste from that of our domestic product. Frankly, I prefer our own version, but on occasion, especially during the height of the season, the change to the blanched vegetable is refreshing. Here's how its done.

HARDINESS: Perennial, very hardy.

WHEN TO PLANT: In early spring, when ground is workable.

SPACING: Set plants 18 inches apart in rows 2 feet apart.

DEPTH: Initially from 6 to 8 inches.

HARVEST TIME: The second year, harvest sparingly; the third year, harvest all you like until July 4.

HOW TO GROW ASPARAGUS: Asparagus, considered by many to be the king of vegetables, is among the first spring vegetables to grow in your garden. Plan on an area about 20 feet square, or a row from 50 to 75 feet long for a family of five or six persons. Should you care to can or freeze a supply, a larger plot will be necessary. Unfortunately, top-quality asparagus will not grow in the Deep South because the vegetable needs winters cold enough to freeze the ground at least several inches down. You may have some luck growing asparagus in Virginia, the Carolinas, or Kentucky, especially if you live in an area with a high elevation.

Any well-drained fertile soil is good ground for asparagus. Plan on locating your patch in full sun. Preparing the bed requires a reasonable amount of work, but keep in mind that once planted, your asparagus bed will produce for twenty-five to thirty years.

TO START AND MAINTAIN AN ASPARAGUS BED:

1. **DIG AND LINE THE BED.** Dig a trench 14 to 16 inches deep. Save the soil you have removed in a heap nearby. Fill the bottom 6 inches of the trench with rotted manure, leaf mold, rotted leaves, and compost.

2. **ENRICH THE BED.** Add from five to ten pounds of 5-10-5 fertilizer or from 10 to 20 pounds of organic mixture to each 75-foot row. Work in the soil removed until the trench level is 6 inches below the surrounding soil line. Mix the soil, organic matter, and fertilizer with a cultivator.

3. **PLANT THE ASPARAGUS.** You will get quicker and more satisfactory results if you purchase one-year-old asparagus plants from a garden center or through the mail order nurseries than if you plant from seed. If you purchase your plants from a nursery, be sure they are not dried out. They should have a root spread of at least 15 inches, the larger the better. Buy only reliable strains. When the soil is ready for planting, place the crowns of the asparagus at least 1-1/2 feet apart in rows 2 feet apart, and the same distance apart if you plant a bed. Cover the crowns with an inch or two of soil. During the season, as the asparagus spears grow, gradually fill in the rest of the trench until it is at surrounding soil level.

4. **CULTIVATE.** Clean cultivation will encourage growth, so keep your asparagus bed weeded from the start. Hand weeding is probably the best way to do this, but if you use a pre-emergent annual weed killer before the spears appear, the job will be easier.

5. **CUT JUDICIOUSLY AS THE BED IS ESTABLISHED.** Do not cut your asparagus the first year. The second year cut only to the beginning of June. The third year, cut until the beginning of July. Be sure to cut every single spear during the cutting period. Then, allow the asparagus to grow undisturbed. In the fall, remove the dead tops and dispose of them, as they harbor the asparagus beetle.

6. FERTILIZE LAVISHLY. Every spring, either before
or after the cutting season, fortify your 75-foot row of
asparagus with from six to eight pounds of 5-10-5 fertilizer
or your organic mixture. Also add compost or rotted
manure. It is nearly impossible to overfertilize asparagus,
as the plant is a very heavy feeder.

HOW TO BLANCH ASPARAGUS: In Belgium, the asparagus
fields resemble burial grounds for cobra snakes. Mounds of earth
about a foot in height stretch from one end of the fields to the other.
If you want to try blanching asparagus, you must cover your already
established rows before the third-year spears emerge. Place one foot
of very friable soil on top of each row. Each mound should be about 1
foot wide at the top, and perhaps 1-1/2 feet wide at the bottom. As
soon as cracks appear in the top of the mound, you can assume the
asparagus is ready for cutting. Gently move some of the earth
mound to be sure. Then insert a very long knife into the mound
about 9 or 10 inches below the top and cut. Pull the spear out of the
soil and re-firm the mound with your hands. I strongly suggest that
if you wish to grow blanched asparagus, you start out on a small
scale. Mound about 10 feet of your established row to see if you
enjoy the blanched variety as well as the green. If you do, you can
always mound more of your row the following year. And then, if
you don't care for it, you can remove the 10-foot-long mound in fall.

GARDENER'S TIP 1

Fertilize, fertilize, fertilize. It is the secret to a bumper crop.

GARDENER'S TIP 2

Be sure your cutting tool is razor sharp so that you don't disturb
the rest of the plant.

GARDENER'S TIP 3

Again, and most important, once the bed is established, do not cut
after the beginning of July.

GARDENER'S TIP 4

Once you have ceased cutting and let your plants grow to their seasonal maturity, be sure to cut off all stalks bearing berries just below the berry line. This assures that the strength of the plant will not go into producing seeds, but rather will develop a stronger root system.

GARDENER'S TIP 5

Remove any seedlings which may have sprung up in or near your asparagus patch. The offspring may not grow true to their parents. Offspring may harbor asparagus rust, which will affect your plants negatively.

PESTS: Asparagus rust and asparagus beetles are chief enemies of the plant. Rust-resistant varieties are the answer to avoiding the disease. Asparagus beetles can be picked off the plants by hand.

VARIETIES: Jersey King and Jersey Knight are two recently introduced cultivars developed by Dr. Howard Ellison of Rutgers University. They yield almost twice as many spears as the old Mary or Waltham Washington strains. Crowns are all-male hybrids which resist all major asparagus disease, and yield is substantially better.

COOKING TIP 1

A considerable number of food experts in the world consider the cuisine of Belgium superior to that of France. One of the classic recipes of Belgian cuisine is *Asparagus de la Flamande*, in which tender white spears are presented with a sauce. Here's how you make it: To make the sauce, crush four hard-cooked eggs in a small bowl. Add 1 cup melted butter, 2 tablespoons minced parsley, and 1 tablespoon fresh lemon juice or 1/8 teaspoon freshly ground nutmeg. Salt and pepper to taste. Serve the sauce in a sauce boat along with about 1 pound of the steamed blanched asparagus. You can also serve this sauce with our American green asparagus.

COOKING TIP 2

At family gatherings in Belgium, the hard-cooked egg is served on a plate. Each person takes one and mashes it himself. The other ingredients are served in a sauce boat and passed around for each diner to sprinkle on his mashed egg and asparagus.

ASPARAGUS BEANS

(Vigna unguiculata)

These Chinese vegetables are different in taste from our domestic pole beans. They have a zippy, nutty, pea-like taste which some liken to that of asparagus. Actually, they are not a member of the bean family, but of the cow pea family. And the nice thing about them is that the plants keep bearing all summer long and into the fall, as long as you continue to pick them as they form. They also freeze well for winter use.

HARDINESS: Annual, tender.

WHEN TO PLANT: In late spring, mid-May to early June, when all danger of frost is over. Like other bean seeds, these will rot in cool, damp weather.

SPACING: Like domestic pole beans, plant around a 6-foot pole, about 2 inches apart.

DEPTH: One to 2 inches.

HARVEST TIME: Around 45 to 55 days after planting and then throughout the summer and fall until a killing frost.

HOW TO GROW ASPARAGUS BEANS: Cultivation is the same as for domestic pole beans. Like most vegetables, these require full sun and a reasonably fertile soil. Do not feed heavily, but a side dressing of 5-10-5 fertilizer or organic mixture will do no harm. Just sprinkle a handful around the base of the plants once they have emerged. Hammer your 6-foot pole into the ground before you plant the beans. Then dig a circle about 1 to 2 inches in depth and plant the seeds 2 to 3 inches apart. Cover with soil and tamp down. When the seedlings are 2 to 3 inches high, pull out every other one. Cultivate to keep free of weeds throughout the growing season and water deeply during drought.

GARDENER'S TIP 1

As with all beans, rabbits are perhaps your chief enemy. Be sure to enclose your garden with fence.

GARDENER'S TIP 2

Pick young for the most tender and flavorful vegetables. Check your plants daily, as these vegetables grow substantially overnight.

GARDENER'S TIP 3

Do not cultivate these beans when morning dew is on them. Bean rust, if present, will spread.

GARDENER'S TIP 4

Sometimes these seeds take up to a month to germinate. Do not despair if the seedlings have not emerged after 2 weeks. Be patient.

GARDENER'S TIP 5

At the end of the season, and before killing frost, let some of the plants fully mature. Then pick the pods, dry them, and remove the seeds for next year's crop.

GARDENER'S TIP 6

Most experts agree that inoculating bean and pea seeds before planting ensures good plant growth, which in turn results in higher yields. The process sounds complicated but it isn't at all. Simply purchase some inoculant from your garden center and proceed as follows. Moisten the seeds, pour on the inoculant powder, roll the seed in the powder, coating it generously, and plant the seed. The inoculant is a bacteria powder that helps the seed do its job of taking nitrogen from the air and storing it in the plant's root nodules.

PESTS: Apparently there are none.

VARIETIES: Asparagus Bean, Dow Gauk, or Yard-Long Bean.

COOKING TIP 1

These beans are delicious stir-fried. Cut them in 1-1/2 inch lengths. Stir-fry 1 minute. Add 2 tablespoons water. Cover 2 to 3 minutes.

COOKING TIP 2

Asparagus beans are also deliciously refreshing when pickled. To prepare, marinate 1 pound beans in 2 tablespoons salad or olive oil, 2 tablespoons water, 2 tablespoons cider vinegar, some grated onion, and some fresh dill. Let sit in the refrigerator overnight and serve chilled.

Beans

....

Haricots Verts or French Beans

(Phaseolus vulgaris)

In France, there is no such thing as "French-cut" green beans. The reason is that an entirely different kind of bean from the American variety is grown and favored. And with good reason, for French haricots verts (filets) are very thin, delicate vegetables. To put it simply, they taste better than ours. In this country, they occasionally appear on menus of elegant hotels or restaurants, but generally are imported from France and thus are astronomical in price. Ten dollars for a small side dish is not unusual. You can have them on your table all summer long and, if you freeze your surplus, during the winter as well, for there is absolutely no trick to growing them. If you have grown such domestic varieties of snap beans such as Tender Pod or Top Crop, you can grow these—the culture is exactly the same. The two things that you must know to grow them is a source of the seed, and when to harvest the beans.

HARDINESS: Annual, tender.

WHEN TO PLANT: After all danger of frost from mid-May to early June, as bean seeds react badly to cool, damp conditions. Then, every 2 weeks for successive crops.

SPACING: Rows about 2 feet apart. Plant seeds about 2 to 3 inches apart.

DEPTH: About 1 inch.

HARVEST TIME: 45 to 55 days after planting.

HOW TO GROW HARICOTS VERTS: Beans require full sun and will grow well in any moderately fertile soil. Generally, heavy feeding is not necessary, although a side dressing of 5-10-5 fertilizer or organic mixture won't hurt. With a hoe, make a row 1 to 2 inches in depth and plant the seeds 2 to 3 inches apart. Cover with soil and tamp down. Cultivate to keep free of weeds throughout the growing season and keep well watered during droughts. About 6 weeks later you will notice scores of very thin string beans developing on the bushes.

Gardener's Tip 1

Rabbits, chipmunks, and other nibbling creatures relish small bean plants, so unless you take precautions, you may have little left for yourself. They must be enclosed by a fence.

Gardener's Tip 2

The secret to harvesting these beans is to pick them when they are very young. Do not wait for them to grow to the thickness of domestic varieties. They should measure perhaps 1/4 inch across and 4 inches in length. Try to pick your beans every day, for your plants will produce more beans if you do. Do not wait for them to grow to the size of domestic beans.

Gardener's Tip 3

There is an old maxim that states: do not cultivate haricots verts when the morning dew is on them. I experimented and found that, yes, the maxim is true. Bean rust is easily spread at that time.

Gardener's Tip 4

Inoculate your bean seeds before planting, if you haven't grown beans successfully there before. Simply purchase some inoculant from your garden center and proceed as follows. Moisten the seed, pour on the powder, roll the seed in the powder, coating it generously, and plant the seed. The inoculant is a bacteria powder that helps the plant do its job of taking nitrogen from the air and storing it in the plant's root nodules.

PESTS: Mexican bean beetles and bean leaf beetles are the only pests. Both can be controlled with a 5 percent rotenone WP (5 table-spoons to 1 gallon of water).

VARIETIES: Fin de Bagnols, Roi Belges, Triomphe de Farcy, Nickel, and a new addition, Radar. The advantage of Radar is that the beans are borne higher up on the plant, producing a cleaner vegetable and one easier to pick.

COOKING TIP 1

Avoid doing exotic things to these choice morsels. Simply boil or steam them and serve with butter. If you can avoid salt, do so, as the delicate flavor of these beans will be more readily savored.

Here is the classic French way of cooking these vegetables. Fill a very large pot with water, add salt, and bring to a rapid boil. Then pour in the haricots verts and boil rapidly uncovered. When the beans are al dente, that is crisp to the bite, about 8 to 10 minutes, remove them and plunge them in ice water.

COOKING TIP 2

Another way the French use haricots verts follows: Cut the beans into half-inch lengths, cook them al dente, and marinate them in oil, vinegar, and shallots for a simple but elegant accompaniment to a summer lunch or dinner.

ROMANO BEANS

(Phasolus vulgaris)

These are the beans that northern Italians use in cooking. They are fleshier and more intensely flavored than our domestic varieties. Again, as with so many gourmet vegetables, there are no tricks to growing them. If you can grow domestic string beans, you can grow Romano beans.

HARDINESS: Annual, tender.

WHEN TO PLANT: In late spring, mid-May to early June, when all danger of frost is past. Like other beans, Romanos rot in damp, cool soil. Then plant again every 2 weeks for successive crops.

SPACING: Rows 2 feet apart. Plant seeds about 2 to 3 inches apart.

DEPTH: 1 to 2 inches.

HARVEST TIME: 6 to 7 weeks.

HOW TO GROW ROMANO BEANS: Plant in full sun in moderately fertile soil. At planting time, work a little 5-10-5 fertilizer or organic mixture into each row before you sow the seeds. Use a hoe to make a row about 1 inch in depth and plant the seeds 2 to 3 inches apart. Cover with soil and tamp down. Throughout the growing season cultivate to keep free of weeds, and water well during droughts. About 50 days later, when the beans are about 4 -1/2 inches in length, pick them. Cook them or freeze for use later.

GARDENER'S TIP 1

Protect against rabbits, who will make mincemeat out of seedlings when they emerge.

GARDENER'S TIP 2

Do not allow Romano beans to grow old, as they become tough and quite inedible.

GARDENER'S TIP 3

Cultivate beans only in the heat of the day.

GARDENER'S TIP 4

Romano beans are not hybridized, so at the end of the picking season, allow several plants to grow to maturity. Then, when the pods are dry, pick them, shell them, and use the seeds for next year's planting.

GARDENER'S TIP 5

All legumes benefit from inoculation before planting the seeds, at least the first few times. Purchase an inoculant from your local garden center, moisten the seeds, pour on the powder, roll the seed in the powder, and plant.

PESTS: Mexican bean beetles, which are oval and copper-colored, and bean leaf beetles, which are red to yellow with black spots, may attack your plants. Hand-pick or use a 5 percent rotenone WP (5 tablespoons to 1 gallon water).

VARIETIES: Roma.

COOKING TIP 1

The Romans prepare these as follows: For 3 pounds of beans, 2 tablespoons of minced onion are sautéed until translucent. Two tablespoons of olive oil are added to the skillet, followed by the beans, salt and pepper, and 1/3 cup water. Simmer until tender about 6 to 7 minutes, drain, and serve immediately.

Belgian Beets

(Beta vulgaris)

Americans have developed some delicious beets, including the golden variety that is surprisingly tasty. But the Belgians grow strains that are at their flavorful peak when less than 1 inch across. As with so many of these Epicurean treats, there is no special cultivation needed. If you can grow standard Detroit or Harvard beets, you can grow these Belgian varieties.

HARDINESS: Annual, hardy.

WHEN TO PLANT: Early spring, when ground is workable.

SPACING: Rows 14 inches apart, six seeds per foot.

DEPTH: 1/2 to 1 inch.

HARVEST TIME: 7 to 8 weeks.

HOW TO GROW BELGIAN BEETS: Plant early in full sun, as beets do not thrive in hot weather. And plan on putting in another row or so every 2 weeks to ensure a good supply for the table through most of the summer. First, to encourage rapid growth, remove all stones, twigs, and other trash from soil. Mix in 3 pounds of 5-10-5 fertilizer per 100-foot row or 6 pounds of your organic mixture plus compost, lime if needed, and rotted manure. Beets also respond well to wood ashes, so if you burn wood in your fireplace or stove, save the ashes during the winter and add to the soil in spring. They are approximately 50 percent lime.

Using the handle of your hoe or rake, dig a furrow no more than 1 inch deep and drop the seeds in six per foot. If your soil bakes to an impenetrable surface after light rain, cover the seeds with a mixture of peat moss and sand instead of soil. Keep the seedlings well watered and remove weeds by cultivating. Mulch with grass clippings, straw, or sawdust. Remember that the latter two draw nitrogen from the soil. Return it by fertilizing during the growing season.

When the small roots begin to penetrate above the soil, probably in 7 to 8 weeks, check the size of the beets to determine whether or not they are ready for harvesting. Ideally, they should measure about 1 inch in diameter.

PESTS: Two pests attack beets. Leaf spot will cause small round spots with light-colored centers on the leaves. Crop rotation will help to cut down on this problem. Leaf miners may also attack beets. These are yellow creatures about 1/8 inch in length that tunnel within the leaves. Other than interplanting insect-repellent plants such as garlic, herbs, marigold, and nasturtium, maintaining a clean garden, relying on birds, reptiles and friendly insects, there does not seem to be a non-hazardous way to rid yourself of these pests. Two teaspoons of malathion to 1 gallon of water should be sprayed on the leaves as soon as any evidence of the insect is noticed. Do not spray for 7 days before harvest.

VARIETIES: Pronto and Chiogga, which are both mini beets; and Golden, a yellow beet with a very deep beet flavor.

COOKING TIP 1

Should you have to thin the beets to 6 per foot, the beet greens which you pull can be prepared like spinach. Cook them with the least amount of water for the best flavor and most nutrition. Simply wash the leaves and put them in a heavy saucepan with a little water still clinging to the leaves. Cover the pan and place it over moderate heat. The leaves wilt quickly and provide their own water for cooking. Check them after 5 to 7 minutes—texture should still have some body. Some people like to drain the cooked leaves, chop them coarsely, and add them to a skillet with a little minced onion, coarse salt, chopped bacon, and a dash of olive oil, then sauté. These tips hold true as well for spinach and chard and for other tasty thinnings.

COOKING TIP 2

Aside from the usual beet with orange glaze or beets with dill, you can also prepare these beets with sour cream as they do in Middle Europe. Here's how you do it. Take 2 cups of boiled beets, sliced or whole, and add 2 tablespoons butter, 1 tablespoon lemon juice, 1/2 teaspoon salt, a dash of freshly ground pepper, 3/4 teaspoon caraway seed, and 1/4 cup sour cream. Place all ingredients in a saucepan and heat, but do not boil. Serve immediately.

BELGIAN CARROTS

(Daucus Carota var. sativus)

Our California carrots are indeed splendid, but you've probably seen packages of tiny orange carrots imported from Belgium in the frozen food section of your supermarket. Well, you can grow them at home as easily as domestic varieties. But, after about 6 weeks, be sure to pull several to see if they are ready to eat, as these carrots must be harvested young to be at their best.

HARDINESS: Annual, hardy.

WHEN TO PLANT: In early spring, as soon as ground is workable, and every 2 weeks for successive crops.

SPACING: Rows about 1 foot apart. Sow tiny seed thinly—ultimately you will have to thin the plant to 2 to 3 inches apart.

DEPTH: 1/2 inch.

HARVEST TIME: 8 to 10 weeks.

HOW TO GROW BELGIAN CARROTS: Perhaps the most important thing to remember when preparing your carrot bed is to remove all rocks and debris from the soil. If you do not, chances are the roots will be deformed when you pull your crop. Since these vegetables are very small, you won't have to prepare the soil too deeply; however, if your soil is heavy, you might consider adding sizable quantities of vermiculite or, even better, perlite to the soil to lighten it, thus creating a more favorable medium. Work in compost, rotted manure, and 5-10-5 fertilizer or organic mixture.

To plant the seeds, pick a spot in full sun. Make a shallow furrow with the end of a hoe or rake and plant the seeds about 1/2 inch deep. Keep the bed well watered and cultivated throughout the growing season. You will probably have to spend some time hand-weeding between the plants. When seedlings are about 2 inches high, thin to every 2 or 3 inches. After 6 weeks, pull several carrots to determine if they are ready for harvest. If they measure about 3 to 4 inches long and perhaps 1/2 inch to 3/4 inch across they are ready for eating, cooking, or freezing.

Gardener's Tip 1

To facilitate planting the tiny seeds, mix with sand before sowing.

Gardener's Tip 2

Carrot seeds are very slow in germinating, so don't worry if several weeks pass before you see the tiny green shoots emerging from the soil. Many gardeners mix radish seed with their carrots in order to mark the rows and to harvest a double crop from the same garden area. Radish is ready for harvest in about 3 weeks from planting time, so by the time you've pulled your radishes, the carrots will be ready to claim the space.

Gardener's Tip 3

During dry spells, water thoroughly, as carrots need a great deal of moisture to develop properly.

Gardener's Tip 4

In the case of carrots, the biggest is not the best, unless of course you plan on making hatchet soup. (Hatchet soup was made in pre-Revolutionary Russia by soldiers stranded in Siberia. It consisted of boiling water, one immense carrot, one very large potato, and one monumental turnip with a rusty hatchet thrown in to add some color.) No! Pick them small and enjoy them.

PESTS: Carrots are generally pest-free; however, you may have a problem with carrot caterpillars, though they are seldom so numerous that you can't hand-pick them. To avoid leaf blight, rotate crops and avoid excessive moisture. Wireworm, a yellowish white worm with dark head and tail, 1/2 to 1-1/2 inches long, tunnels into stems and roots; plant winter rye and turn under in the spring. The soil bacteria which attack the rye are thought to attack the wireworms.

VARIETIES: Thumbelina, Kinko, Babette and Minicor.

Cooking Tip 1

At Le Pigeonneau, a charming inn in Aix-en-Provence, France, carrots are julienned, combined with julienned potatoes, and deep-fried. The resulting crunchy nest of vegetables is topped with a dollop of spinach stuffing just before serving. The colorful orange of the carrots and golden brown of the potatoes is very appealing to the eye, and the combination of tastes quite special.

BELGIAN ENDIVE

(Cichorium intybus)

Quite probably the most elegant of all salad vegetables,
Belgian endive is a member of the chicory family, as is radicchio, another bitter but elegant salad leaf. The pale, furled
"chicons" of Belgian endive which are so refreshing in salads
can be grown in your garden and either forced in situ or
indoors where winters are very severe. Considering the price
of a single small head of it, it is worth the little trouble to do
so. All of the endive available in all of the markets all over the
world is grown in Belgium.

HARDINESS: Biennial.

WHEN TO PLANT: For forcing Belgian endive, allow three
months of growing before the first frost, which is the time you dig
the roots for the second stage of growing. So, subtract three months
from the first frost date in your area and plant at that time. The
summer solstice, June 21 is a good time to plant in most parts of the
country.

SPACING: Thin to 1 foot apart in rows 1 foot apart.

DEPTH: 1/4 inch.

HARVEST TIME: After second stage of growing (See below), when
shoots appear above soil line in containers.

HOW TO GROW BELGIAN ENDIVE: Shepherd Ogden, owner
of the Cook's Garden mail order nursery, an excellent source for all
sorts of gourmet vegetables, suggests this method of growing and
forcing endive:

> **1. PLANT.** Plant seeds in a spot in full sun with a
> well drained soil fortified with organic matter.
>
> **2. DIG.** Before ground freezes in the fall, dig plants
> root and all. Store harvested roots in a cool place in
> damp sand until ready to use.

3. FORCE. To force the roots, trim them to 8-10 inches long, stand them neck to neck in containers or boxes of moist sand or peat, and water lightly but regularly.

4. ALLOW TO SPROUT IN THE DARK. Keep in complete darkness at 50-60 degrees F and 95 percent humidity (a black plastic bag with holes poked in it is an easy way to do this.

5. HARVEST. Harvest the sprouts (called chicons), when they are 4-6 inches tall by cutting just above the crown. With good care, they will resprout for a second (and even third) crop. They mature in from 60 to 150 days.

Gardener's Tip 1

Before planting, when you fortify soil with compost or enriching additive, be sure to sift medium, as stones or chunks of organic matter will impeded proper growth of roots.

PESTS: Slugs and snails are the only problem. Place pie tins full of beer near the plants. Creatures will climb into the pie plate to drink the beer and drown in it.

VARIETIES: Flash, Turbo, Witloof Zoom, and Robin.

Cooking Tip 1

Among their other attributes, the Belgians are thought by many to be the best cooks on earth. And, they are responsible for growing almost all of the endive available all over the world. They use it in many ways, both fresh and cooked. Braised endive is an exceptionally delicious dish. You do this by gently browning the endive in butter in a skillet and then covering the vegetable with chicken stock, simmering until tender.

Cooking Tip 2

The classic endive salad is made with the leaves of this elegant vegetable, some chopped pickled beets, and a simple oil and vinegar dressing.

COOKING TIP 3

Another very elegant salad is made with the cultivar called Robin, which has a pale pink tinge to it after forcing. Serve it raw, with peeled slices of a tart apple such as Granny Smith, and cover with a raspberry vinegar salad dressing.

COOKING TIP 4

When grilling an outdoor meal in summer, add chicons of Belgian Endive to a medley of grilled vegetables. Toss thick slices of sweet red peppers, sliced red onions, Beligan endives, whole mushroom, cherry tomatoes, and slices of anise root in seasoned olive oil, wrap loosely in heavy aluminum foil, and toast on the grill till they are smoky and just fork tender. You can approximate the same effect in winter using the top rack of a 400° oven. Open the foil to expose the vegetables to the caramelizing heat.

BOK CHOY

(Brassica rapa pekinensis)

If you cook in the Chinese manner, you know that bok choy is basic to Oriental cuisine. It is easily grown as a spring crop, if you know where to get the seeds. Bok choy, like lettuce and spinach, will bolt in hot weather, so plant in early spring or for a fall crop.

HARDINESS: Annual, very hardy.

WHEN TO PLANT: In early spring, as soon as the ground is workable, or late summer.

SPACING: In rows 1 foot apart. Sow ten seeds per foot. Thin to 6 inches apart.

DEPTH: 1/4 inch.

HARVEST TIME: About 45 days, when bok choy is 10 to 14 inches tall, just before plant flowers.

HOW TO GROW BOK CHOY: Plant as soon as the ground is workable, or in the cold weather of autumn. Bok choy likes full sun, reasonable moisture, and a fertile soil fortified with rotted manure, compost, and some 5-10-5 fertilizer or organic mixture. Plant the seeds in full sun about 1/4 inch deep and sow them about ten to the foot. The seeds will germinate in about 10 to 15 days. When the seedlings are 3 inches high, thin to 6 inches apart. Fertilize lightly every 2 weeks or so with a side dressing of 5-10-5 fertilizer or organic mixture. After about a month you will be able to cut some of the loose green leaves from the plant. Later you can cut the center stalk or heart. One nice thing about bok choy is that through the cutting season the plant will replenish itself. New leaves and a new heart will grow from the cuttings. When the heart of summer arrives, bok choy will bolt to seed.

GARDENER'S TIP 1

Rabbits relish bok choy, so be sure to enclose with a fence.

GARDENER'S TIP 2

Be sure to allow one plant to go to seed. The seed forms in a pod. When it is dry, crack it open, remove the seeds, and store in a cool, dry place for sowing in the fall or the following spring.

PESTS: Other than rabbits, few pests attack bok choy.

VARIETIES: Several, all non-hybrid. They're all good.

COOKING TIP 1

In China and Japan, people dry a substantial amount of their bok choy crop for use during the winter. When the plant is mature, and before it goes to seed, pull it out and remove the roots. Leave the leaves on the plant, but you can remove the tender heart for immediate use. Wash the vegetable, boil it for 5 to 10 minutes, then hang it up on the clothesline to dry for 5 to 6 days. Each night, bring the crop into the house and cover it with plastic. When it is dry, wrap it and store in a cool, dry place.

COOKING TIP 2

Bok choy is delicious in egg drop soup. After you've heated 1 pint chicken broth, add 3 tablespoons cornstarch diluted in 1/4 cup water. Heat and stir until soup is clear. Bring to a boil and add sliced stems of bok choy. Then add 1 beaten egg and stir. Finally add chopped bok choy leaves to the soup. Coarsely chopped bok choy is also delicious in cream of potato soup, along with a dash of ground cayenne and some extra garlic. Chunks of leftover baked ham will gild the lily. Add the bok choy toward the end of cooking so it retains some body. You wish to avoid a slippery texture.

Cooking Tip 3
I have also substituted bok choy for celery in a cold bay scallop salad. The taste is infinitely more subtle than celery, permitting the delicate taste of the scallops to dominate the salad.

Broccoli Raab
(Brassica oleracea var. italica)

Only recently has broccoli raab (also called broccoli rape, rabe, rape, rappa, or Romanesco broccoli) become popular in the United States. It has been grown for many years in northern Italy and, although of the broccoli family, it does not have the same growth habit. It forms loose light colored green clusters of heads and has a taste with just a bit more bite than traditional broccoli.

HARDINESS: Annual, hardy.

WHEN TO PLANT: Because broccoli raab needs cool weather to properly set heads, it is best grown as a fall crop. Sow seeds in mid to late summer for a crop 60 days later.

SPACING: In rows 1-1/2 feet apart, thin to about 1 foot apart.

DEPTH: 1/4 inch.

HARVESTING: About 60 days from a mid summer planting to a fall harvest.

HOW TO GROW BROCCOLI RAAB: Plant in mid summer for a fall crop or in fall for late winter-early spring crop if your weather is mild. Full sun is preferred, but partial shade is acceptable. Plant in well fortified soil, and keep well watered during dry, late summer drought periods.

GARDENER'S TIP 1

After the first cutting, wait a few weeks and you can cut a second time, and then a third time.

PESTS: Since it is of the cabbage family, the same pests that attack cabbage attack broccoli raab. That is, cabbage maggots and worms, which can be controlled with organic rotenone, and aphids, which can be blasted off plants with a strong spray of water from the hose.

VARIETIES: Cima di Rapa, Rapini.

COOKING TIP 1

Cut both the tender young leaves and stems just as soon as the stems are about 6-8 inches tall. Sauté briefly in olive oil with minced garlic or shallots and freshly ground black pepper. Top with parmesan cheese. Once the heads flower they are still delicious. Scatter in salad.

CARDOONS

(Cynara cardunculus)

Cardoons, relatives of the artichoke, are rarely grown in this country. Since it is a rather large plant, most vegetable gardeners feel it takes up too much space in the garden for them. However, it is becoming more and more popular as a decorative planting in the landscape. My friend Robert Dash, whose famous garden Madoo is located in Sagaponack, New York, has incorporated cardoons in his landscape plantings. The plant's silvery gray leaves are serrated and sport many reddish thistle-like flowers. Cardoons are grown for their edible stalks in Mediterranean areas, particularly Italy.

HARDINESS: Perennial in mild winter areas (Zone 7-10). In colder climates grow as an annual.

WHEN TO PLANT: In spring after all danger of frost. Start seeds indoors under lights at the same time you start tomatoes in your area. Plant seedlings 3-4 feet apart.

SPACING: 3-4 feet.

DEPTH: Sow seeds 1/4 inch deep in seed-starting containers. When you plant them outdoors, plant at soil level of container in which they were started.

HARVEST TIME: If perennial in your area, you can start to pick stalks in mid summer. If grown from seed, harvest in the fall, when stalks have matured.

HOW TO GROW CARDOONS: Plant in full sun, in rich, well-fortified soil. Water regularly and deeply during summer dry spells.

Gardener's Tip 1

For best eating, stalks must be blanched (like cauliflower, celery and blanched asparagus). This is a somewhat tedious task, but it is essential to the edible cardoon. When the plant has grown to three feet, grab stalks and hold them together in an upright position. Then place a rubber band around the top of the stalks. Then wrap the bunch of stalks in burlap or paper bags. About 4 weeks later, harvest stalks at soil line and cut off tops of stalks which are green and have grown above the blanching area.

PESTS: Aphids may attack. Spray infected areas with a strong jet of water from the hose. If slugs and snails attack, as with artichokes, place a pie pan of beer close by. Slugs will climb into the beer and drown.

VARIETIES: Simply cardoon.

Cooking Tip 1

After blanching and harvesting, the edible part of the vegetable is creamy white, looking somewhat like celery heart. Use only blanched stalks. Remove stringy parts of each one and rub with lemon juice to prevent them from turning black. Gently simmer in chicken broth for about 1-1/2 hours or until fork tender. There are many ways to prepare them for the table. After simmering, the French cover them with Mornay, hollandaise, mousseline or butter and cream sauce (see any standard cookbook for recipes), sprinkle with grated parmesan cheese, dot with a little butter, and either heat in a 450° oven, or glaze under the broiler.

COOKING TIP 2

The Italians prepare cardoons in many different ways, but here's a very easy treat, a refreshing salad for summer. Cut up blanched cardoons, arrange in a bowl and season with your favorite salad dressing. Garnish with chopped parsley and chervil.

BEET GREENS

(Beta vulgaris)

Few American cooks know that beets provide the cook not only with the bulbous beet, but also with foliage which is quite delicious. So, you get twice the pleasure from this classic vegetable.

HARDINESS: Annual, hardy.

WHEN TO PLANT: In early spring, when ground is workable.

SPACING: Rows 14 inches apart, six seeds per foot.

DEPTH: 1/2 to 1 inch.

HARVEST TIME: 4 weeks.

HOW TO GROW BEETS FOR GREENS: See instructions for growing Belgian beets. Culture is exactly the same.

GARDENER'S TIP 1

Be sure to pick leaves when quite young, as they will be sweet and tender. If you wait beyond four weeks from planting, they tend to become very strong in flavor and less tender.

PESTS: Two pests attack beets. Leaf spot will cause small round spots with light-colored centers on the leaves. Crop rotation will help to cut down on this problem. Leaf miners may also attack beets. These are yellow creatures about 1/8 inch in length that tunnel within the leaves. Other than interplanting insect-repellent plants such as garlic, herbs, marigold, and nasturtium, maintaining a clean garden, relying on birds, reptiles and friendly insects, there does not seem to be a non-hazardous way to rid yourself of these pests. Two teaspoons of malathion to 1 gallon of water should be sprayed on the leaves as soon as any evidence of the insect is noticed. Do not spray for 7 days before harvest.

VARIETIES: Early Wonder is the variety to select for greens.

COOKING TIP 1

When you're thinning your beets to six plants per foot, be sure to save the greens for the table. Either add them to a salad or cook them as you would spinach.

COOKING TIP 2

A classic Belgian and French dish is to combine the leaves of endive with chopped pickled beets and a simple oil and vinegar dressing. If you use beet greens instead of the chopped beets with the endive, you're in for a treat.

CELERY ROOT

(CELERIAC)

(Apium graveolens var. rapaceum)

The classic French creation Celery Remoulade is made from this white root. It is rarely available in the markets but is easily grown in your garden. Unlike celery, which is somewhat difficult to grow, celery root will thrive if given a reasonable amount of attention.

HARDINESS: Annual, hardy.

WHEN TO PLANT: In early spring, as soon as ground is workable.

SPACING: In rows 1-1/2 feet apart; plant seeds thinly, about 1/2 inch apart, and thin to 6 inches when 3 inches high.

DEPTH: 1/2 inch.

HARVEST TIME: Fall or, if wintered over, very early spring.

HOW TO GROW CELERY ROOT: Allow plenty of time for growing, as celery root requires a long season to mature. Plant in full sun, in early spring as soon as ground is workable—that is, when you plant onions, peas, and spinach. Fortify the soil with plenty of rotted manure, compost, and 5-10-5 fertilizer or organic mixture. The seed is small and requires some time to germinate, so soak overnight in water to help speed the process. To facilitate sowing, mix the wet seed with dry sand and distribute it evenly in your planting row. Sow seeds about 1/2 inch apart, 1/2 inch deep. Cover with soil, tamp down, and lightly sprinkle the bed with water. When the seedlings are about 3 inches high, thin to 6 inches. During the growing season, cultivate and water abundantly during periods of drought. Harvest in the fall, or provide winter protection by banking with soil and covering with piles of dead leaves. Dig during the winter or early spring for fresh celery root.

Gardener's Tip 1

If you wish, in the fall you can dig your celery root crop, cut off the tops, and store the roots in a box of moist sand. Place the box in a cool, dry cellar.

PESTS: Few, if any.

VARIETIES: Brilliant, Diamont.

Cooking Tip 1

A simple but delicious French bistro recipe for celery root follows: Peel and wash the root, then julienne into matchstick sized strips. Sauté julienned root in a tablespoon of butter. Season with a little salt and a little confectioner's sugar. Simmer gently until tender.

CHARD

(SWISS CHARD)

(Beta vulgaris cicla)

Since spinach is often difficult to grow in the home garden, Swiss chard is a fine substitute. Use it as you would spinach and grow it as you would beets, to whose family it belongs. Chard is basically a cool season crop but tolerates higher summer temperatures than spinach without bolting and survives winter temperatures down to 7° F. Mild and delicious chard is both beautiful, with its scarlet stems, and versatile in the kitchen.

HARDINESS: Biennial.

WHEN TO PLANT: In spring as soon as ground is workable.

SPACING: Rows spaced 15-18 inches. Thin to 8-12 inches. Use thinned plants as greens.

DEPTH: 1/4 inch.

HARVEST TIME: Harvest spring-sown crop in summer and late-summer-sown crop all through the winter where winters are relatively mild.

HOW TO GROW CHARD: Select a site in full sun or partial shade and sow seeds directly into the garden as soon as soil is workable. Although they are not fussy about soil, and will grow in almost any soil, enriched soil, fortified with rotted compost or manure, will produce a far more satisfactory crop. Water thoroughly during summer drought.

GARDENER'S TIP 1

When harvesting, cut off outer leaves 1-2 inches from ground while tender. Be careful not to injure remaining leaves of the plant.

GARDENER'S TIP 2

The Swiss chard cultivar Ruby has brilliant red stalks, red leaf veins, and is so attractive that it is being used more and more in borders and as an ornamental plant or in porch and patio containers.

PESTS: There are none, save occasional chewing insects which may leave holes in the leaves. But these are harmless.

VARIETIES: Charlotte, Monstruoso, Erbette, Fordhook, Giant Ruby.

COOKING TIP 1

Swiss chard is prepared and served exactly like spinach. The leaves have a very special tangy taste, quite appealing. Some people strip the stalks of the leaves and prepare them like asparagus. Since the stalks cook more slowly than the leaves, it is usually a good idea to separate stalks from leaves and either add the leaves to the cooking pot after the stalks are nearly tender, or prepare the two parts of the plant in different ways. For a delicious potato soup, prepare a simple soup with chicken broth, potatoes, onion, and seasonings. When the potatoes are soft, add a little cream to thicken to taste. Toss in a handful of shredded chard leaves and heat through.

CHINESE CABBAGE

(Brassica rapa pekinensis)

Chinese cabbage is basic to Oriental cooking. It's easily grown as a spring crop. Like bok choy and most other Oriental leafy vegetables, Chinese cabbage cannot abide hot weather, so plant early in the spring or for a crop in the fall.

HARDINESS: Annual or biennial usually grown as annual.

WHEN TO PLANT: In early spring, as soon as the ground is workable, or late summer.

SPACING: In rows 1 foot apart. Sow six seeds per foot and thin to 6 inches apart.

DEPTH: 1/2 inch.

HARVEST TIME: About 80 days, before plants bolt.

HOW TO GROW CHINESE CABBAGE: Plant the seeds in a sunny spot in the spring as soon as the ground is workable, about the same time you plant lettuce, peas, and onion. Fortify the soil with rotted manure, compost, and 5-10-5 fertilizer or organic mixture.

Plant seeds about 1/2 inch deep, in rows 1 foot apart. Sow six seeds per foot; when the plants are 3 inches tall, thin to 6 inches apart. Lightly fertilize with 5-10-5 fertilizer or organic mixture about every 3 weeks during the growing season. As the plants grow larger, tie the leaves together to blanch the vegetable. Of the two varieties, siew choy and ya choy, ya choy is the sweeter vegetable.

GARDENER'S TIP 1

Chinese cabbage will bolt in hot weather, so plant early and pick before going to seed. Let one plant go to seed and collect the seeds for next year's planting.

PESTS: Flea beetles and leaf hoppers may attack the leaves of your plants. Nontoxic natural rotenone will control these. Aphids can be attacked with a peppery spray from your hose.

VARIETIES: There are two types of Chinese cabbage, the Napa, or headed variety and the open head type. Summer Top or Blues are the Napa varieties to select. Lettuce is the open head type.

COOKING TIP 1

Obviously, Chinese cabbage can be used as you would domestic cabbage—i.e., raw in salads or stir-fried. But for a special treat, prepare a Chinese Lion's Head soup, so named because of the large meatballs it contains. Chinese cabbage is the most important and preponderant ingredient. This soup, by the way, is an excellent choice for a buffet dinner, for atop a fire in a chafing dish, the texture and consistency remains constant. Consult any comprehensive Chinese cookbook for recipe.

COOKING TIP 2

Last spring I gave some seeds of Chinese cabbage to my friends the Haralambou family, originally from Cyprus. They used the cabbage instead of grape leaves to wrap the classic Greek meat and rice—and found that the Chinese cabbage was much more tender than grape leaves.

COLLARDS

(Brassica oleracea acephala)

The famous greens of the American South, collards can be grown all over the country. With their somewhat strong cabbage flavor, they are not to everyone's taste, but do complement chicken and ham favorably.

HARDINESS: Annual, hardy.

WHEN TO PLANT: Sow seeds thinly directly in the garden as soon as soil is workable, several weeks before last frost. Sow again in mid-summer for a fall crop.

SPACING: Rows about 2 feet apart. Thin to 1-1/2 to 2 feet.

DEPTH: 1/4 inch.

HARVEST TIME: Pick leaves as soon as plant is established. If planting for fall, pick leaves after frost as cold exposure tends to improve flavor.

HOW TO GROW COLLARDS: Select a site in full sun with average soil. Plant seeds in early spring. Keep well watered during summer drought.

GARDENER'S TIP 1

Remember that collards are much improved in flavor by cold weather. So, if possible plan on planting them in mid summer rather than as a spring crop.

PESTS: Since collards are of the cabbage family, they attract the same pests. Cabbage maggots and cabbage worms can be controlled with organic sprays such as rotenone. If aphids attack, blast them with a water hose. Or rub them off with your hands.

VARIETIES: Flash, Champion.

COOKING TIP 1

Boil or steam the cabbage-like leaves. For a gourmet touch, dress them up with chopped onion, and a little bit of olive oil, and vinegar.

CRESS

(PEPPERGRASS)

(Lepidium sativum)

Cress (garden cress or peppergrass) is a peppery cousin of watercress. It is easily grown, and you can even cultivate it indoors on a bed of cotton or felt. Its zesty tang brings springtime right to your table. And it is a splendid substitute for the water-grown variety.

HARDINESS: Annual, very hardy.

WHEN TO PLANT: In early spring when ground is workable, then successively every 2 weeks throughout the season.

SPACING: Rows about 1 foot apart; plant seeds thinly.

DEPTH: 1/4 inch.

HARVEST TIME: About 10 days after planting.

HOW TO GROW CRESS: Plant in full sun or semi-shade as soon as ground is workable and then about every 2 weeks for a continuous supply of young leaves. Sow the tiny seeds rather thinly, about 1/4 inch deep. To facilitate this, mix the seeds with sand before sowing. Cover with fine soil and keep moist until seeds germinate. You should be able to start picking in about 10 days. Plant successive crops every 2 weeks.

GARDENER'S TIP 1

At the end of the season, be sure to let some of your cress go to seed so that you will have a supply for the following season. Store seeds over the winter in a cool, dry, dark place.

PESTS: There are none.

VARIETIES: Curlycress, Broadleaf, Curly.

COOKING TIP 1

Cress is ideal for the tiny finger-size tea sandwiches greatly favored in England and on the Continent. Simply take thinly sliced white bread, remove the crusts, butter lightly, and fill with cress.

Cornichons
(Gherkin Pickling Cucumbers)

(Cucumis sativus)

Gherkins are cucumbers with short fruits that are harvested young and used mainly for pickling. The resulting cornichons, or gherkin pickles, are served with patés and lemon wedges on the continent. They are available in the markets, usually imported and quite expensive. You can grow them as easily as you grow domestic cucumbers and put them up yourself. They make very attractive gifts to give to friends at Christmas time, and they'll taste better than any you can buy.

HARDINESS: Annual, tender.

WHEN TO PLANT: After danger of frost, mid-May to early June.

SPACING: In 1-foot-wide hills, spaced 2 1/2 feet apart. Plant five to seven seeds per hill.

DEPTH: 1/2 inch.

HARVEST TIME: About 60 days.

HOW TO GROW GHERKINS: Plant in full sun, in mid-May or early June, when all danger of frost is past. All cucumbers prefer a fertile, light, well-drained soil, so add well-rotted manure or organic matter to your cucumber hills. Also add side dressings of 5-10-5 fertilizer or organic mixture once the plants have started to grow. Mound up your soil to a height of about 6 inches and a width of about 1 foot. Plant from five to seven seeds in a small circle around the center of the hill. When seeds have germinated, thin from three to five seedlings per hill. Keep well watered during the season, as cucumbers thrive on plenty of water.

If garden space is at a premium, you can grow cornichons in a row, if you provide netting or wire fence as support. Simply train the runners up the support. You will not need to support individual fruits with slings, as they are small. When the fruit begins to develop, check your crop each day, as cucumbers grow very fast. Pick when no longer than 1-1/2 inches in length for best results.

GARDENER'S TIP 1

A mulch beneath your cornichon patch will help to conserve water and keep your vegetables from contact with the soil, which will cause them to be green on one side and yellow on the other. Black plastic, grass clippings, or salt hay will help to conserve water, warm the soil, and impede rot.

GARDENER'S TIP 2

Remember to pick these every day, for once overgrown fruit appears on the vines, the plant will stop producing.

PESTS: Striped cucumber beetles are your main enemy. They are yellow to black in color with three black stripes down their backs. They grow to be about 1/5 inch long and feed on leaves, stems, and fruit. Hand-pick the beetles or use rotenone spray (5 tablespoons to 1 gallon water) or 1 percent rotenone dust. Squash vine borers, which are white and up to 1 inch long, can also be controlled to a certain extent with rotenone. The usual control, however, is to slit the stem with a knife when the borer is located and to cover the leaf nodes with soil to induce rooting all along the stem. Squash bugs are brown with flat backs. Colonies are usually visible. In the evening lay down some boards near the plants. In the morning, lift up the boards and collect the gathered bugs.

VARIETY: West India Gherkin.

COOKING TIP 1

Several excellent recipes for pickling gherkins appear in *Larousse Gastronomique*. You will find that recipes calling for uncooked gherkins will result in a more crisp, fresher-tasting little pickle.

COOKING TIP 2

As a quick substitute for cold paté, use cold meatloaf. Serve very cold with gherkin pickles and slices of lemon. Your guests will never guess that it's leftover meatloaf. Surprisingly, the French love American meatloaf. They do not prepare it at home, and can't seem to get enough of the stuff. My friend Sue Blair, while living in Paris, always served cold meatloaf at summer dinner parties. With gherkins and lemon slices, it was a smashing success. She became so famous for her meatloaf that in a recent book about the world of Paris high fashion, the chapter about her was entitled "Meatloaf Again."

DANDELION

(Taraxacum officinalis)

Although you can eat the very young leaves of wild dandelion, the cultivated variety is infinitely more tasty, and a treat indeed. And, it is quite easy to grow. It is standard table fare in France, Belgium and Italy, but except for ethnic areas in the United States is almost non-existent as a salad or cooked green.

HARDINESS: You can plant as an annual in spring, but dandelion is tough, and if you plant in the fall, it will survive very cold temperatures, spring up in late winter, and provide greens for salads by mid-spring.

WHEN TO PLANT: As soon as ground is workable in early spring. Or in early fall for a spring crop.

SPACING: Rows about 1 feet apart. Plant seeds about 2 to 3 inches apart. Thin to 9 inches.

DEPTH: About 1/4 inch.

HARVEST TIME: 45 to 55 days after spring planting, or if you have sown in the fall and wintered over, when leaves are about 6-8 inches long.

HOW TO GROW DANDELION: Plant in rich, fortified soil in full sun or partial shade. Keep well-watered during dry spells.

GARDENER'S TIP 1
As plants grow, pinch off all flower heads. This will force growth into leaves and roots of plant.

GARDENER'S TIP 2
The leaves of dandelion are bitter, and so are blanched for kitchen use and a sweeter flavor. Tie the leaves together in a bunch so that light does not affect lower leaves.

PESTS: There are none, except occasional rabbits who nibble at the leaves.

VARIETIES: Amerliore is the most widely grown. It is French and "improved"—that is, it tastes much sweeter than older traditional varieties.

COOKING TIP 1

Beyond use as a salad green, dandelion can be cooked like spinach, and used in the same way in cuisine.

EGGPLANT

White or Japanese (Solanum Melongena var. esculentum)

These smaller, more tender, and delicately flavored cousins of our domestically grown purple variety will make an eggplant addict out of anyone with the slightest preference for this vegetable. And these are not more difficult to grow than our domestic eggplants.

HARDINESS: Annual, tender.

WHEN TO PLANT: Since eggplant needs a long growing season, start plants indoors about 8 weeks before planting season, which is mid-May to early June.

SPACING: Indoors: 1/2 inch apart; outdoors: Plant seedlings 2 feet apart in rows 2 feet apart.

DEPTH: Indoors: 1/2 inch; outdoors: At soil line of plant.

HARVEST TIME: Anywhere from 100 to 140 days after sowing.

HOW TO GROW WHITE EGGPLANT: Since a long growing season is necessary to ripen this vegetable, start indoors about 8 weeks before you plant tomatoes and peppers outside in your area. Plant the seeds 1/2 inch deep in containers. On top of 2 inches of potting or garden soil, spread about 1/2 inch of vermiculite or sphagnum moss. Then plant the eggplant seeds about 1/2 inch deep. Water thoroughly and cover the containers. As the plants grow, transplant them to separate containers such as peat pots or cut-off milk cartons and fill with a good garden loam. Place your plants in a south window and keep well watered. After about 6 weeks, begin to harden the plants off by placing them outside on warm, sunny days. Then about 1 week before planting, leave the plants out overnight if the temperature is not too cold. The following week transplant them into the garden in a spot that receives full sun. But be sure to select a gray day, as the hot sun may burn and wilt the young seedlings.

Your soil should be rich, so fortify with several wheelbarrow loads of manure or rotted compost per 50-foot row. Also add about 5 pounds of 5-10-5 fertilizer or 10 pounds of organic mixture to each row.

Dig shallow holes about 2 feet apart for your plants and fill them with water. When the water has settled in, place your plants in the soil and fill up the hole with soil.

Be sure to fashion collars of aluminum foil, cardboard, or tin cans to place around your plants when you set them in. These will ward off cutworms. Firm the soil around the roots. This will leave a slight depression, which will serve to catch water. If during the next day or so the sun is inordinately strong and the plants wilt, simply water well and provide some sort of temporary shade for them. Control weeds during the season and water thoroughly during drought. Harvest these eggplants when they are only 2 inches in diameter.

GARDENER'S TIP 1

Chances are your plants will set more fruit than the plant can reasonably produce. When the initial blossoms have set and fruit begins to form, pinch off all later blossoms. In that way, your plants will produce vegetables of quality rather than in great numbers.

GARDENER'S TIP 2

To avoid weeding, lay down a mulch of black plastic, grass clippings, or salt hay.

GARDENER'S TIP 3

Out here where I live on the far eastern end of Long Island, the farmers grow potatoes, hence the Colorado potato beetle is quite prolific. Eggplant attracts them, so if you are not prepared to hand-pick the beetles or spray with rotenone, avoid this crop.

PESTS: To avoid blossom-end rot, those dark, sunken leathery spots at the end of the fruits, water well during the early growing stages. Leaf miners can be controlled with 25 percent Diazinon EC, but keep in mind that this chemical is toxic.

VARIETIES: The newest offering is Tango which is ready for harvest in just 60 days.

COOKING TIP 1

Here's an easy way to prepare this vegetable when you are barbecuing teriyaki steak or chicken. Simply cook the entire unpeeled eggplant alongside over slow coals until soft, about 10 minutes on each side. Serve with grated daikon or grated ginger root and soy sauce.

ESCAROLE
(ENDIVE)

(Cichorium endivia)

In this country escarole is often called endive or French endive, though it is quite a different thing from what we call Belgian endive, witloof, or witloff French endive *(Cichorium intybus)*, which is the forced "chicon" of another member of the chicory family. Endive and chicory are frequently listed as the same item in plant catalogues. In spite of the popular confusion that seems to surround its nomenclature, escarole is a vigorous and delicious plant, very useful in mixed salads where it adds distinctive taste.

HARDINESS: Annual, very hardy.

WHEN TO PLANT: In early spring, as soon as ground can be worked.

SPACING: Rows about 1 foot apart. Plant seeds 1/2 inch apart and thin as season progresses to about 8 inches apart. Successive plantings every 10 days or so will ensure a summer-long supply.

HARVEST TIME: Anywhere from 3 to 7 weeks (3 weeks for first thinning to 7 weeks before bolting).

HOW TO GROW ESCAROLE: Plant in late March or early April as soon as the ground is workable. Escarole likes full sun, abundant moisture, and a reasonably fertile soil, so fortify with compost, rotted manure, and handfuls of 5-10-5 fertilizer or organic mixture spread along the rows. Sow the seeds thinly about 1/2 inch deep, cover with soil, tamp down, and keep moist. After about 3 weeks you can start to thin out your escarole, adding the tiny leaves to salads. Continue to thin out as the season progresses until the heads stand about 8 inches apart. Plant successive crops every 10 days or so until the heat of summer. Escarole will bolt in heat, making it bitter and inedible. Plant again in early September for a fall crop.

PESTS: Escarole is relatively pest-free.

VARIETIES: Green Curled, Broad-Leafed Batavian (often listed in plant catalogues under "Endive").

COOKING TIP 1

If you plant a fall crop of escarole you can cut the heads after the first frost; tie the outer leaves around the heads to blanch the centers, and store them in a cool, dark place. The vegetable will keep that way for as long as a month. Escarole adapts very well to soup recipes calling for chicory or endive. A cream of escarole soup recipe worth investigating appears in the *Larousse Gastronomique*.

FENNEL

(Foeniculum vulgare var. dulce)

Fennel, or sweet or Florence fennel (sometimes called by its Italian name, finocchio) is surely one of the most versatile of vegetables. Its leaves impart a delicate anise flavor to soups, salads, fish, and eggs. The stalks are delicious when mature, and the dried seeds collected in the fall can be used in confections and baked goods. Rarely available in markets, except perhaps in Italian neighborhoods, fennel or finocchio is easily grown in your garden.

HARDINESS: Annual, tender.

WHEN TO PLANT: After all danger of frost, from mid-May to early June.

SPACING: In rows 1-1/2 feet apart, sow seeds about 1/2 inch apart, thinning to about 8 inches.

DEPTH: About 1/2 inch.

HARVEST TIME: Leaves can be picked in midseason, stalks later on, and seeds in late fall.

HOW TO GROW FENNEL: When you plant your beans, it is time to plant fennel, that is, in mid-May or early June. Fortify the soil with rotted manure, compost, and 5-10-5 fertilizer or organic mixture and plant in full sun. Plant seeds about 1/2 inch apart, 1/2 inch deep, and when seedlings are 3 inches high, thin to 8 inches. Cultivate and water throughout the season. After about 2 months, some of the leaves can be removed from each plant for use in salads or soups. Then in September, when the stalks are broad and white, they can be used as a prepared vegetable. Let some plants go to seed in the late fall. Collect the seeds and use them in sweets or when you bake rolls or bread. Be sure to save some for planting next season.

GARDENER'S TIP 1

The strong anise odor of finocchio repels many insects from other vegetables.

PESTS: Fennel is pest-free.

VARIETIES: Sweet Florence, Neapolitan, Romy, Supewadremen, Fennel Fino, and Zefa Fino are recommended.

COOKING TIP 1

Mediterranean people all enjoy fennel. The Italians first parboil the stalks in water and then sauté them in butter, adding grated Parmesan cheese when they are done. The vegetable is often served with roast pork with bay leaves. The Greeks use fennel in salads, mixing it with olives, feta cheese, onions, and lettuce.

GARLIC

(Allium sativum)

During the past decade, garlic has become one of the most popular of all vegetables to grow in the garden. No longer do gardeners have the choice of old-fashioned garlic or elephant garlic. Both of which are excellent incidentally. The taste of these recently available varieties is a shade sweeter, and/or hotter than that of conventional garlic. Growers describe their garlic varieties as either hardneck or softneck. Hardneck garlics send up a central stalk, which you should remove as soon as it appears on the plant, and softneck garlics have lost the ability to produce a central stalk, thus producing a larger garlic bulb.

HARDINESS: Annual or biennial, very hardy.

WHEN TO PLANT: In early spring when ground is workable or in the fall with winter protection.

SPACING: Rows 1 foot apart. Plant sets 6 inches apart.

DEPTH: With pointed tops about 1/2 inch below surface of soil.

HARVEST TIME: Late August, early September.

HOW TO GROW GARLIC: For maximum size, you must plant the cloves in the fall. Then, protect through the winter with a hefty covering of mulch leaves and mounded earth. Plant the cloves blunt side down, about 6 inches apart, with the tops about 1/2 inch below the surface of the soil. Space your rows 1 foot apart. Be sure to select a spot in the garden that receives full sun. Fortify the soil with plenty of compost, rotted manure, and some 5-10-5 fertilizer or organic mixture. The following spring, remove your winter covering and cultivate to assure a weed-free patch. In late August or early September, when the leaves have turned brown, dig the garlic and place the bulbs on a screen in the sun to dry. Be sure there is adequate ventilation during this period. The following week, cut off the tops, rub the dead leaves, skin, and dry soil off the bulbs, and store them in a cool, dry place. Each garlic bulb will produce about one dozen cloves.

GARDENER'S TIP 1

You can plant garlic in the spring, at the same time that you plant onions and shallots, but the bulbs will not grow to full size. If you choose to do this, follow cultivation instructions for shallots.

GARDENER'S TIP 2

As with shallots, another member of the Allium, or onion family, be sure to save the largest cloves from your fall crop. Either plant them in the fall or save for the spring.

GARDENER'S TIP 3

If you plant a great deal of garlic in your garden, you will have little trouble with insect pests.

PESTS: There are none.

VARIETIES: Hardneck garlics are easier to peel than softnecks, and offer many subtle gradations of taste. Some varieties offered are:Pitarelli, Brown Saxon, Bogatyr, Romanian Red. Softneck garlics tend to be hotter with a more narrow range of tastes. Some varieties are: Chefs Italian Red, Inchelium Red, Creole Red, Early Asian Purple Skin, Spanish Roja.

COOKING TIP 1

As you know, if you love garlic, you'll try to put it in everything you eat. Here's a suggestion for garlic lovers. If you've traveled in the Mexican countryside, you've undoubtedly sampled their garlic soup. It's easily prepared at home. Just heat about 1 quart chicken broth, add 2 minced garlic cloves, a dash of salt, and some freshly ground black pepper; simmer for about 10 minutes. Pour boiling hot soup into warmed bowls at the table and break a fresh egg into each bowl of soup. The egg will poach right in the bowl.

GINGER ROOT

(Zingiber Officinalis)

Those who enjoy Chinese or Indian cuisine know that fresh ginger root is essential to them. You can grow it in a pot in your house. It's easily raised and makes a fine addition to your houseplant collection. If you decide to grow ginger root, you will not only have a free, steady supply of this spice but a handsome plant and, if you're lucky, flowers as well.

HARDINESS: Very tender; grow as houseplant.

HOW TO GROW GINGER ROOT: To grow ginger root, buy one in the market. The root is a gnarled, knobby rhizome, brown outside and pale yellow inside. This is what you plant and ultimately use in cooking. Choose a healthy specimen, one that is firm and plump with a shiny skin. Soft wrinkled ginger roots will rot in a pot.

To plant the root, fill a 6-inch container with a mixture of one part potting soil, two parts sand, and one part humus or peat moss. Be sure to place gravel or flower pot shards in the bottom of the container for drainage. Bury the ginger root just below the soil surface and thoroughly soak the container with warm water.

Place the pot in a south window or, barring that, a west window. If you have only eastern or northern exposure in your house or apartment, grow ginger plants under lights, as they need plenty of sunshine. If the house or apartment is dry in the winter, spray mist daily. Keep your plant evenly moist throughout the growing season.

In several weeks, green shoots will emerge, growing ultimately to a height of about 2 1/2 to 3 feet. Leaves of the plant are elongated and are placed alternately on the stem, arranged in two vertical rows. Your plant may have to be staked at this point.

If conditions are ideal—that is, if the plant receives enough light and moisture—the ginger plant may flower. Blooms are borne on leafless stems from 6 to 12 inches high and are formed in dense cone-like spikes. The spikes are about 1 inch thick and from 2 to 3 inches long, composed of overlapping green bracts which may be edged in yellow. Each bract encloses a small yellow-green and purple flower.

Now for the harvest. When the roots have completely filled the container, that is, when the plant is potbound and roots are seen emerging from the drainage holes at the bottom of the container—it is time to harvest.

Remove the plant, shake the dirt off, and wash the roots. Cut off a 2- or 3-inch part of the new root system to start another crop. Discard the original part of the root which was planted.

To store ginger root, either keep it in a dry, cool place, freeze, or place in an airtight container, cover it with sherry wine, and store in the refrigerator. It will keep indefinitely. You will not need much of this spice to prepare exotic dishes, as ginger is strong and peppery.

PESTS: There are none.

VARIETIES: Simply ginger root.

COOKING TIP 1

Ginger root is as basic to Oriental cooking as salt and pepper is to Western cuisine. However, there are many Chinese and Japanese fish dishes which include a spicy ginger and scallion sauce. Consult any Chinese or Japanese cookbook for more information.

HORSERADISH

(Amoracia rusticana)

Why settle for the bottled variety, when home-grown horse-radish is infinitely more pungent and tasty? There are no tricks to growing horseradish, and it is virtually indestructible.

HARDINESS: Perennial, hardy.

WHEN TO PLANT: In early spring when ground is workable.

SPACING: Rows 1 foot apart, root cuttings 1 to 2 feet apart.

DEPTH: To soil line on plants, usually between root and crown.

HARVEST TIME: From spring through fall as needed, but spring diggings are best.

HOW TO GROW HORSERADISH: Either purchase stock from a garden center or mail order nursery or purchase a root in the market and cut it into root cuttings. To do this, cut the root into pieces 6 to 8 inches long, the thickness of a lead pencil, and plant in full sun. Horseradish can also be propagated from crown cuttings. Merely cut a piece of the root and crown bud from a specimen and plant. Spring is the best time to do this. Dig a trench 4 to 5 inches deep and place the cuttings at an angle with their tops near the surface of the ground. Usually new roots will develop during the first year. Once established, pieces of roots and crowns remaining in the soil after harvest are usually sufficient to reestablish the plants.

GARDENER'S TIP 1

Since horseradish is a perennial plant, select a site in your garden away from the annual Rototilling. Also, be sure to keep the plants in check, as horseradish can be invasive, spreading rampantly.

PESTS: There are none.

VARIETIES: New Bohemian.

COOKING TIP 1

Horseradish sauces are served as accompaniment to many meats and fish. Combine it with whipped cream and serve with smoked fish or boiled beef.

COOKING TIP 2

Although grated horseradish combined with grated beets is a standard condiment in Eastern Europe, most Americans have never tasted it. It is served with traditional Easter hunt breakfasts in Poland and Russia and is easily prepared: combine 1/2 cup grated horseradish with 1 cup grated cooked beets, 4 tablespoons white vinegar, 1 tablespoon sugar, and 1 teaspoon salt. Store in the refrigerator. It will keep for about 1 month. It is excellent with hard-boiled eggs and cold smoked ham.

KIPFEL KARTOFFEL
(FINGERLING POTATOES)

(Solanum tuberosum)

These diminutive yellow-fleshed potatoes are well known to gardeners and gourmets throughout Europe. They grow about 1 inch in diameter, several inches long, and have a flavor and quality all their own. They are not porous or mealy in texture as common table potatoes, but waxy and firm, producing a potato salad unexcelled. Today Kipfel Kartoffel are grown commercially in Austria, but because the local demand is so great, exporting seed potatoes is against the law. In other words, the only way you can eat these in the United States is if you grow them yourself. They require a little more effort than most crops, but are indeed worth the time.

HARDINESS: Annual, hardy.

WHEN TO PLANT: Between the end of March and April 15, when the soil is friable and not too muddy. Later in the far northern reaches of the country.

SPACING: About 1-1/2 feet apart.

DEPTH: 6 to 8 inches.

HARVEST TIME: Late summer.

HOW TO GROW KIPFEL KARTOFFEL: Several days before planting time mix together about 4 gallons of rotted manure, compost, and 2 pounds of 5-10-5 fertilizer or 4 pounds of organic mixture and spread it over a 5-by-10-foot plot. This size plot will ultimately provide you with about half a bushel of potatoes. Plant in full sun. Dig the mixture into the soil to a depth of 10 inches. Several days later, dig furrows 6 to 8 inches deep, in rows about 1-1/2 feet apart. Plant the seed potatoes whole and cover them gently with soil.

When they have grown about 6 to 8 inches high, usually around 3 weeks later, when they have grown another 6 or 8 inches, hill them again to the lower leaves. Cultivate your crop during the summer or mulch with grass clipping, straw, or other material but do not water them. Kipfel Kartoffels do not have the water content of domestic potatoes. In other words, the firmer they are, the better they are.

In the fall, when the tops of the plants have become brown and start to wilt and when the soil is dry, dig the potatoes. Do not dig them after rain or when the soil is muddy. Do not be disappointed at low yield. Kipfel Kartoffel plants produce about 20 to 25 percent of the regular potato yield.

Dry the potatoes for a few hours in the shade. Never put them in the sun. Do not wash, as water causes rapid deterioration of quality.

Store your crop in a cool, dry, dark place, in a bushel basket covered with newspaper. A cellar or unheated garage is suitable. When the deep freeze of winter arrives, store them in a place where they will not freeze. They should keep through the winter.

GARDENER'S TIP 1

Although it is not supposed to work, I did it successfully. Simply store a supply of the potatoes in the refrigerator over the winter and then plant them in the spring.

GARDENER'S TIP 2

Remember not to expose your potatoes to the sun after you've dug them. Although the released poison won't kill you, it will make you quite ill. This, incidentally, is true of all potatoes, for they are members of the nightshade family.

PESTS: Colorado potato beetles may well attack your plants. They are yellow with black stripes on their wing segments. Either hand-pick them off or spray with 5 percent rotenone WP, 5 tablespoons of rotenone to 1 gallon of water.

VARIETIES: Ladyfinger, Yellow Finger, or Kipfel Kartoffel.

COOKING TIP 1

When cooking these potatoes for eating, boil them with the skins on. I have found that if you cut them in half before boiling, you simply squeeze them and the delectable waxy, yellow potatoes come right out of their skins. Kipfel Kartoffels can be eaten in salad or fried as hash browns. But they are not suitable for mashing, French frying, or baking.

COOKING TIP 2

Probably the best potato salad on earth is made from these potatoes. Here's the recipe. Boil about 4 cups of Kipfel Kartoffels as you would the common kitchen potato. After about 15 minutes, test one of the larger potatoes with a cake tester. If it goes in without any difficulty, your potatoes are done. Prepare while the potatoes are still warm. You will notice that they are firm, not porous like common potatoes. For this reason, oils, vinegar, or mayonnaise will not be absorbed if they are cold. The 4 cups of potatoes should yield about 2 cups sliced. Put them in a bowl and add 1 teaspoon minced onion, 2 tablespoons peanut oil, and about 1 teaspoon white vinegar. Salt and pepper to taste. You can also add some chopped parsley, hard-boiled egg, and/or bacon bits if you like. Mix this together and chill to the bone in the refrigerator. I have made the traditional American potato salad with mayonnaise, using these potatoes, but found their delicate flavor overpowered by the mayonnaise.

LEEKS

(Allium porrum)

Ah, the mighty leek. A joy in the kitchen but expensive and difficult to find in the markets. There is a little more work involved in growing this superb vegetable than most, but well worth the time and effort.

HARDINESS: Annual, hardy.

WHEN TO PLANT: In early spring, as soon as ground is workable.

SPACING: Rows 2 feet apart. Thin plants to 4 to 6 inches apart.

DEPTH: 1/2 inch.

HARVEST TIME: 4 to 6 days.

HOW TO GROW LEEKS: You can produce a healthy leek crop in any soil that is neutral or nonacid with good drainage. Full sun is required, along with sufficient moisture and weed-free conditions.

There are two ways to grow this vegetable. You can either start seeds indoors about 6 weeks before early spring planting or sow them directly in the soil at the earliest moment you can dig. The reason for starting indoors is that leeks require a growing season of some 130 days to reach maturity. If you want fresh leeks by the end of summer, you will have to start seeds indoors. If you are willing to wait until late fall, plant seeds directly outdoors later. One advantage of late planting is that with a minimum of protection, leeks will winter over, and in the spring, as soon as the soil thaws out, you can dig fresh leeks for your table.

If you plan on starting seeds indoors, simply plant them 1/2 inch deep in your planting medium. Place the trays in a sunny window and 6 weeks later, when the plants have reached a height of from 6 to 8 inches, transplant into the garden.

Prepare the soil for your bed by adding rotted manure or compost. A scattering of 5-10-5 fertilizer or organic mixture should be worked in as well. Be sure to rake out stones and other debris, as leeks must grow in friable soil in order to form properly.

If you are planting seeds directly into the garden, sow them about 1/2 inch deep. When they are 6 to 8 inches tall, transplant them to another row, following instructions below for seedlings started indoors. When your seedlings are 6 weeks old and ready for transplant, dig them and snip off half of the upper leaf portion. Then dig a furrow about 6 to 8 inches deep. Plant the leeks 4 to 6 inches apart and cover only the soil line. As the leeks grow, fill in the furrow with soil. This will serve to blanch the bottom, edible root portion of the plants. About 3-1/2 months later, when the leek is of considerable size, pull one to see if it is ready for the table. It should resemble a monumental scallion.

GARDENER'S TIP 1

Mulching is a difficult task for leeks-since you mound your rows with dirt to blanch, it is nearly impossible to keep the mulch in place. Cultivate frequently and remove other weeds by hand picking.

GARDENER'S TIP 2

Be sure to leave some of your crop in the ground over the winter. Pile dead leaves or compost over the plants, then after the spring thaw, dig them up for a special early spring treat. You can also winter them over in a cold frame if you wish.

GARDENER'S TIP 3

Leeks need watering during drought periods. Be sure to give them at least 1-1/2 inches of water a week

PESTS: Generally leeks, like other members of the onion family, are pest-free. If onion maggots strike, use 57 percent Malathion EC (2 teaspoons to 1 gallon of water). These worms bore into the bulbs, causing them to shrivel. Thrips are yellow to brown, winged, very active, and about 1/25 inch long. They cause white blotches to appear on the leaves, which eventually wither and die. The same Malathion solution will arrest the destruction. Be sure to follow instructions for using this chemical to the letter. There are some hazards involved in its use.

VARIETIES: Varna, King Richard, Pancho, Tadorna and Laura.

COOKING TIP 1

For a very elegant fish course, prepare a basic fish mousse mixture out of about 1 pound of sole or flounder fillets. Then cut the base off of 3 leeks and separate the leaves. Wash 12 or 14 of the largest leaves and parboil for about 6 minutes. Trim leek leaves into rectangles about 9 inches long, place about 3 tablespoons of the uncooked mousse on each, and roll into tidy pockets. Place the pockets seam down in a buttered baking pan, 8 inches by 14 inches, along with 5 tablespoons clam juice. Dot with butter, cover with aluminum foil, and bring to a boil on the range. Then bake in a preheated 400-degree oven for 15 minutes. Serve immediately with a beurre blanc sauce.

COOKING TIP 2

An easy, and yet very elegant way to prepare leek, is to braise it. Cut root off of bottom of leek. Cut away green part at top, leaving only the white. Cut these into pieces about 4 inches long. Half them and tie each with some string, so that they don't fall apart. Sautè lightly in butter. Cover with chicken broth and simmer slowly (about half an hour). As leek cooks, broth will evaporate, eventually becoming a golden brown syrup. This is what you want. If too thick simply add more chicken broth a tablespoon at a time, until it is the consistency of maple syrup. You can reheat this if you wish to make it ahead of time.

Lettuces

(Lactica sativa)

You've undoubtedly long since tired of our American super-market iceberg lettuce, and know about Romaine and Bibb lettuce, sometimes available in the markets. But there are dozens of delectable varieties of lettuce which are available only from your own garden. American varieties such as Buttercrunch, Green Ice, Black-Seeded Simpson, and Salad Bowl are all excellent, but beyond that there are many other varieties which are even more tempting. All lettuce is easily grown, relatively pest-free, and a treat in the salad bowl. And, to make this very utilitarian vegetable even more tempting, there are three basic types of lettuce. First there is head lettuce, which grows in tight little heads; leaf lettuce, which produces crisp, crinkly, or curly-leafed specimens; and cos or romaine lettuce, which develops tightly folded leaves that grow in an upright manner.

HARDINESS: Annual, hardy.

WHEN TO PLANT: For spring lettuce, in early spring, as soon as ground is workable, for summer lettuce in mid-summer and for ìwinterî lettuce in the fall.

SPACING: In rows about 1 foot apart, sow seeds 1/2 inch apart and thin as the season progresses to about 8 inches apart.

DEPTH: 1/2 inch.

HARVEST TIME: From 3 to 10 weeks—3 weeks for first thinning, 10 weeks before bolting.

HOW TO GROW GOURMET LETTUCE: Plant as soon as ground is workable in the spring. Lettuce prefers full sun, abundant moisture, and a reasonably fertile foil, so fortify with compost, rotted manure, and a sprinkling of 5-10-5 fertilizer or organic mixture. Sow seeds thinly, about 1/2 inch deep, and cover with soil. Tamp down and keep moist until seeds germinate. Plan on planting successive crops every 10 days or so in order to ensure a longer season. After several weeks you will be able to start thinning your lettuce bed, enjoying the plants you pull in salad. Continue to thin heading and cos varieties until plants stand about 8 inches apart. Leaf lettuce can stand about 6 inches apart. It needs a great deal of water and to be shaded somewhat from the hot sun. For fall lettuce, when cool weather returns to your area in early September, plant a fall crop.

Gardener's Tip 1

This is gourmet food for rabbits, so be sure to fence in your lettuce patch.

Gardener's Tip 2

Part of the secret of extending the lettuce season well into the summer is to be sure that your bed is well watered almost daily during extreme hot or dry spells. It doesn't work, but it is worth a try. You can also cover part of your crop with lattice to provide some shade.

Gardener's Tip 3

Since lettuce generally bolts by mid-July, interplanting with later fall vegetables or even tomatoes can conserve space.

Gardener's Tip 4

Do not pick lettuce before ten o'clock in the morning. Studies have proved that the leaves are higher in vitamin content after that hour. If your lettuce is not as crisp-looking later in the day, simply drench it in a pot of ice water. It will crisp up nicely.

PESTS: Cabbage loopers and aphids may be troublesome. Pick the loopers by hand and use a peppery spray from your garden hose to dislodge the aphids.

VARIETIES

SPRING: Ballon, a large pale European romaine; Freckles green romaine flecked with wine red markings; Four Seasons (Mervielle des Quatre Saisons), a French variety which is sparkling burgundy with tender pink and cream interiors; St. Blaise, small light bright green Romaine; Tango, deep green heavily savored rosettes, Red Grenoble, shiny wine red leaves, Reine des Glaces, exceptionally beautiful with deeply notched leaves and frosty green head.

SUMMER: Apollo, one of the most heat resistant of all, medium green romaine type; Buttercrunch, a Bibb type lettuce that is very heat resistant; Kinemontpas, a French classic for summer; Diamond Gem, trouble-free, slow to bolt, can be grown for hearts of Romaine. Craquerelle du Midi, and openhearted French Cos type of lettuce that is one of the most heat tolerant of all.

FALL AND WINTER: Brune d'Hiver, delicately bronzed, pale green butterhead type, one of the hardiest of all; Rougette du Midi (Red Montpelier) small red butterhead, very hardy; Winter Marvel winter hardy in Vermont, this butterhead winters over under glass and produces large pale green heads very early in the spring.

COOKING TIP 1

Braised lettuce is truly a luxury because it usually takes from 8 to 12 heads of lettuce to make it. However, with an ample garden supply, you need not think about cost of the vegetable. Remove tough outer leaves, tie lettuce with string, and simmer very slowly in chicken broth. When tender serve with some good French wine and a loaf of crispy bread.

COOKING TIP 2

Lettuce will crisp up nicely and will keep for several days in the refrigerator. First wash it, then dry it well—spinning it dry in a salad spinner is a good method—and place it in a zip-top plastic bag in the refrigerator.

Lily Buds

(Hemerocallis)

If you cook in the Chinese manner, you know that lily buds are an ingredient often used in the preparation of this cuisine. Growing your own is foolproof, as these plants are virtually indestructible. Cultivated varieties are called daylilies. You may already have some in your garden, but were not aware that the buds are indeed edible and very delicious at that.

HARDINESS: Perennial.

WHEN TO PLANT: From spring to summer.

SPACING: Set plants about 2 feet apart.

DEPTH: Soil level of plants.

HARVEST TIME: In late spring when buds form, before flowers open.

HOW TO GROW LILY BUD: You can buy daylilies (*hemerocallis*) in your local nursery, order them from mail order houses, or simply dig a clump of the wild orange daylilies which grow roadside in many parts of America. Plants should be divided into stock about 6 inches in diameter. Plant in full sun or partial shade, and forget about them. They are maintenance-free, with an attractive growing habit and handsome foliage. In the late spring, pick the buds before they bloom and dry them. Simply tie together in bunches, hang upside down to dry in a cool, dry, shady place. When they are thoroughly dry, remove the buds from the stalks and store in airtight containers in a cool, dark, dry place.

PESTS: There are none.

VARIETIES: They come in many colors and make welcome, maintenance-free additions to your flower garden.

Cooking Tip 1

Dried lily buds are basic to Chinese hot and sour soup and are often combined with cloud ear mushrooms in various meat and poultry dishes. They are also very good raw or deep-fried as tempura.

Mâche
(Corn Salad)
(Valerianella locusta)

Mâche, a salad green very popular in Europe, is generally eaten during the hot months of summer and early fall when lettuce is unavailable in the garden. Start thinning after 3 weeks and use leaves in salads.

HARDINESS: Annual, hardy.

WHEN TO PLANT: In early spring with successive plantings every few weeks.

SPACING: Rows about 1 foot apart, plant seeds 1/2 inch apart, and thin as season progresses to about 6 inches.

DEPTH: 1/2 inch.

HARVEST TIME: 3 to 6 weeks after planting and then throughout the summer.

HOW TO GROW MACHE: Plant in early spring and then every 2 weeks until fall. Several varieties are cold-resistant and will continue to flourish well into autumn. Mâche likes full sun, firm soil, and plenty of moisture during the summer months. Sow seeds about 1/2 inch apart and 1/2 inch deep and thin to about 6 inches.

PESTS: There are none.

VARIETIES: Big Seed, Green Full Heart, Green Cambrai.

COOKING TIP 1

You've probably never eaten this vegetable, let alone cultivated it, but I urge you to try it. Fresh green salad material in the heat of summer is difficult to come by in your garden. Mâche will satisfy your needs. Here is a recipe for summer mache salad. Combine mache with red leaf lettuce, endive, head lettuce, oil, Roquefort cheese, fresh cream, and cumin to taste. Not only does it taste good, but it is eye-appealing as well.

MUSTARD GREENS

(Brassica rapa)

Mustard greens are full of vitamins, and for the most part are grown only in southern American gardens. They are also very popular in Europe. They add zip to any salad.

HARDINESS: Annual, tender.

WHEN TO PLANT: As soon as ground is workable in early spring. Then every two weeks until late spring. Like many varieties of salad greens, Mustard Greens are a cool weather crop, so do not fare well during hot summer months.

SPACING: Rows 2 feet apart. Thin to 12 inches between plants.

DEPTH: 1/2 inch.

HARVEST TIME: 35 days after planting.

HOW TO GROW MUSTARD GREENS: Sow seeds directly in the garden as soon as soil is workable. Use a site which is in full or partial sun, with very fertile soil, enriched with compost or rotted manure. Since mustard greens are a cool weather crop, drought is usually not a problem; however if it is an exceptionally dry spring, be sure to water.

GARDENER'S TIP 1

Pick leaves when young and tender. Do not use leaves which are partially brown or yellow, as these are over the hill. When weather turns hot, leaves of mustard will become tough and harbor an unpleasant smell, so remove them from the garden.

PESTS: Cabbage maggots and cabbage worms may attack. It is quite rare, but if cabbage maggots or cabbage worms attach, control with an organic substance such as pyrethrum or rotenone.

VARIETIES: There are many: Red Giant, with a taste similar to French Dijon-style mustard, Coquille, a French variety, with cupped leaves, Southern Curled, the traditional Southern United States version, d'Etampes, large round leaves. This variety is cold tolerant and can be overwintered.

COOKING TIP 1

Use in salads or do as they do in the South, steam them and serve with oil or butter as a hot vegetable.

MELON CHARANTAIS

(Cucumis melo)

Many American varieties of cantaloupe or muskmelon are truly superb in texture and flavor, but if you've ever traveled to France during high summer or early fall and sampled the superb Charantais variety, you probably remember it as the most delicious you've ever tasted. And then, if you grow your own melons, you can pick them vine-ripened. As you know from growing your own tomatoes, there is simply no comparison with the supermarket version. These melons are smaller than ours, so don't be dismayed if they don't look like domestic varieties. But wait until you taste them!

Up to now, there has been a small problem in their cultivation because varieties available in this country have not
been resistant to fusarium wilt. Cantaloupe Ido was introduced
last year and is resistant to the disease. You won't regret
investing the little extra effort to grow these choice melons.

HARDINESS: Annual, tender.

WHEN TO PLANT: After all danger of frost, from mid-May to
early June.

SPACING: 1-1/2-foot-wide hills spaced 3 feet apart. Plant five to
seven seeds per hill.

DEPTH: 1/2 inch.

HARVEST TIME: 80 to 85 days.

HOW TO GROW CHARANTAIS MELONS: Plant in mid-May
or early June when all danger of frost is past. Melons, like cucumbers
and squash, are planted in small mounds measuring about 1-1/2 feet
across. They prefer full sun. Dig a small hole about 6 inches deep and
1 foot across and fill it with rotted manure and compost. Then build
up your hill to about 6 inches in height. Plant from five to seven
seeds in a small circle around the center of the hill. When seeds have
germinated, thin from three to five seedlings per hill. Keep well
watered during the season, as melons thrive on lots of water.

GARDENER'S TIP 1

In France, Charantais melons are pruned to produce a better-tast-
ing and earlier-setting fruit. Here's how you do it: When the plant
has two sets of leaves, that is the cotyledons (the first set which
grows and is not characteristic of the true leaves) and the first set of
true leaves, remove the cotyledons. When the plant has grown two
more leaves, pinch out the middle shoot. This will force the vines to
grow out diagonally from the main stem. Then, when each of the
two side vines have produced three or four leaves, pinch the end
again. These side vines will then produce secondary vines which
should be pinched in the center when they have produced two to
four leaves. Finally, when the plant has set fruit, allow only three to
four melons per plant to develop. You don't have to do this, but if
you do your melons will be of superior quality.

Gardener's Tip 2

Most novices don't know when to pick melons. They are ripe when the stem separates easily from the vine. Just pick a melon up in your hand and move it around gently. If it separates from the vine, it is ripe and ready to pick. If not, wait a day or so and repeat the process until it does separate.

Gardener's Tip 3

If space is a problem, plant your melon seeds in a row and train them to grow up a fence or trellis. As the melons develop, fashion slings out of cloth and secure them to the fence.

Gardener's Tip 4

A mulch beneath your melon patch will help conserve water and keep your melons from contact with the soil, which may impede ripening.

Gardener's Tip 5

Protect from rabbits, birds—and believe it or not, turtles! They'll walk miles to taste your melons. In addition to the fence around my garden, I also protect my melons with pieces of chicken wire placed over individual specimens.

PESTS: As with cucumbers, striped cucumber beetles are your main problem. They are yellow to black in color with three black stripes down their backs and grow to about 1/5 inch long. They feed on leaves, stems, and fruit. Hand-pick the beetles or use rotenone spray (5 tablespoons to 1 gallon of water) or 1 percent rotenone dust. Squash vine borers are white, up to 1 inch long, and are also controlled with rotenone. Squash bugs are brown with flat backs. You can spot colonies of these devils. At sundown, lay boards down near the plants. The bugs will spend the night under the boards. Early in the morning, lift them up, collect, and dispose of the bugs. Also, hoe soil over the leaf nodes to induce additional rooting and counter the attacks of the vine borers.

VARIETY: Charantais, the French classic; Alienor, an early Charantais type; Savor, finest flavor of all Charantais melons; Galia, a Mid East type melon with firm fruit. Flavor is reminiscent of bananas; Earlisweet, a honeydew type melon; Snow Charm, pure white to green, an Oriental melon. Compact vines.

COOKING TIP 1

These days the world of sorbet and sherbet has expanded dramatically. Many are made of exotic fruits such as papaya, kiwi fruit or passion fruit. Cantaloupe serves as well. Consult a basic cookbook for a fresh sorbet or sherbet recipe and substitute cantaloupe for the fruit called for. Keep in mind that recipes for sherbets made from fruit juice rather than fruit pulp will not serve as a guide. Serve the sorbet or sherbet with slices or balls of cantaloupe which have been marinated in a small quantity of Kirsch. This dessert is delightfully refreshing and very low in calories.

MIZUNA
(JAPANESE CABBAGE)

(Brassica rapa japonica)

Mizuna, also called Japanese cabbage, is a vegetable of the mustard family. It has a feathery look and is much milder than other mustards. And, it is very slow to bolt during the hot days of summer. It is quick growing, has good clear taste, and after cutting re-groups vigorously.

HARDINESS: Annual, hardy.

WHEN TO PLANT: As soon as ground is workable in early spring. Then every two weeks until late spring. Like many varieties of salad greens, Mizuna is a cool weather crop, so does not fare well during hot summer months.

SPACING: 12 inches apart in rows 2 feet apart.

DEPTH: 1/4 inch.

HARVEST TIME: In early summer. For later crops, sow every two weeks.

HOW TO GROW MIZUNA: Sow directly in the garden as soon as soil is workable. Use a site which is in full or partial sun, with very fertile soil, enriched with compost or rotted manure, Since mustard greens are a cool weather crop, drought is usually not a problem, however if it is an exceptionally dry spring, be sure to water.

Pick leaves when young and tender. Do not use leaves which are partially brown or yellow. When weather turns hot, leaves of Mizuna will become tough and harbor an unpleasant smell, so remove them from the garden.

PESTS: Cabbage maggots and cabbage worms may attack. It is quite rare, but if cabbage maggots or cabbage worms attach, control with and organic substance such as pyrethrum or rotenone.

VARIETIES: There is only one: mizuna.

COOKING TIP 1
Use to add zip to summer salads.

OKRA

(Abelmoschus escutlentus)

Because many Americans associate okra with Cajun food or gumbo, some gardeners think that they will not grow in areas outside of the deep South. This is not true. From planting to picking, only 60 days of frost free weather are necessary for a strong crop of okra. The plants are interesting and dramatic with broad leaves.

HARDINESS: Annual, hardy.

WHEN TO PLANT: Because seeds are very hard, like Morning Glory and Moonflower, soak them overnight in warm water before planting. Then sow seeds in ground after all danger of frost.

SPACING: In warm Southern climates thin to from 2-3 feet apart in rows 3 feet apart. In cooler areas, thin to one foot apart in rows 2 feet apart.

DEPTH: 1/2 inch.

HARVEST TIME: 60 days after sowing in most areas.

HOW TO GROW OKRA: Plant in full sun in soil that has been fortified with rotted compost or manure. plants can grow to five feet, so staking may be needed.

GARDENER'S TIP 1

Okra plants have sharp spines, so be sure to wear garden gloves if you are going to work with the plants in some way. Once harvesting begins, pick pods daily or they will become stringy and tough.

GARDENER'S TIP 2

If you leave pods on the plant, they will dry and become brittle. They add a wonderful touch to dried flower arrangements.

PESTS: Okra is pest free, except that sometimes aphids attack. Blast these off the plants with a strong spray of water from the garden hose.

VARIETIES: Cajun Delight, Burgundy.

COOKING TIP 1

I remember as a child, Campbell's Chicken Gumbo was one of my favorite soups. And that's because it had okra in it. I guess I enjoyed the okra because I had never had it before. For whatever reason, my late mother, one of the most superb cooks I have ever known, did not cook in the southern manner. Beyond using okra in soups, gumbos and Cajun cuisine, they are excellent sliced and fried. You can also bread them, as you would Italian eggplant, and fry them that way, and serve them as side dishes, particularly with fried seafood.

COOKING TIP 2

Okra makes a wonderful zingy, crunchy pickle. Use as you would small pickling cucumbers or gherkins, following an okra pickle recipe from a canning book. Some cooks like to pickle their okra with a few small hot red chili peppers for extra zing.

COOKING TIP 3

The sticky substance inside fresh okra—so crucial to a classic gumbo—will thicken any soup or stew to which the okra is added. The amount of thickening depends largely on the okra-to-liquid ratio, but acid foods like tomatoes and tomato juice seem to reduce the sticky effect somewhat. If you desire less thickening effect from the okra, use it whole, trimming only the very top of the stem, and avoid cutting into the tops of the okra pods when preparing them for the pot.

Onions

(Allium cepa)

Ah, the wonderful world of onions. If asparagus is the king of vegetables, then surely onions are queen. Where would cooks be without onions, since they are basic to all fine cuisine? But so many different varieties are cultivated-where does one begin to select? Which are sweet? Which are pungent? Which grow from sets? Which from seeds? Well, here it is all sifted out for you. Onions are divided into two categories: green onions and "keeping" onions. Green onions are dug from the garden as needed through the growing season. "Keepers" are harvested for storage through the winter.

Common onions—that is, the yellow variety found in all markets—are "keeping" onions. They are strong in taste. Yellow Ebenezer, Yellow Globe, and a vestige of the 18th century, Wethersfield Red, are but a few varieties. Ebenezers and Globe sets are commonly available in your garden centers.

Green onions—that is, those harvested during the season and eaten fresh from the garden—include bottle, globe, bunching, and Egyptian walking onions. These are the onions that you will want to grow. They generally do not keep well.

Bottle Onions

Early onions are excellent as scallions; later onions are full grown. Bottle onions are available in two colors, red and white. These are the varieties found braided and hanging in kitchens and restaurants in Europe. They resemble short, fat cucumbers and have the great advantage of slicing evenly, making them particularly useful for homemade relishes. They are not good "keepers," but are delicate and mild in taste and are especially attractive to gourmands. They are considered the aristocrats of the onion family.

HARDINESS: Annual, very hardy.

WHEN TO PLANT: In early spring, as soon as ground is workable.

SPACING: In rows 1 foot apart, ultimately 3 inches apart.

DEPTH: About 1 inch deep.

HARVEST TIME: Throughout season as needed.

HOW TO GROW BOTTLE ONIONS: As soon as soil is workable, in early spring, plant three seeds per inch, about 1 inch deep in rows 1 foot apart in full sun. Fertilize with 5-10-5 fertilizer or organic mixture and water thoroughly after planting. As the seedlings grow, thin to 3 inches apart to allow space for full-size onions. Thin to 1/2 to 1 inch apart for scallions or cocktail onions. These onions are generally fully mature in from 130 to 150 days.

Gardener's Tip 1

During the growing season, pick the flower-bearing stalks off at the base.

Gardener's Tip 2

You might want to try keeping these onions in braids. You may have luck and you may not, but do not expect hem to remain edible until spring. To cure these onions, when you notice that the tops of the bulbs have that dry, transparent skin on them, gently pull them from the ground. Do not cut the green tops off the onions. Lay them on a screen in full sun for about a week and let them dry out. When the stalk at the neck of the onion is completely dry, the onions are ready to air in a shaded area. Let them dry for several weeks and then prepare for storage. Cut the dry greens from the bulbs and store them in meshed onion bags. Or, if you prefer, leave the tops on and braid them. In either case, store the onions in a cool, dry place until ready to use.

PESTS: All onions are relatively pest-free.

VARIETY: Red Torpedo.

GLOBE ONIONS

Globe onions are known in the markets as Bermuda onions. They are round, milder in taste than the common onion, and grow to impressive size in red, white, and yellow. They generally do not keep well. Bermudas are planted from seedlings or sets. Immature white Globe Bermuda Onions can be used as cocktail onions or in stew.

HARDINESS: Very hardy annual.

WHEN TO PLANT: In early spring, when ground is workable.

SPACING: In rows 1 foot apart, ultimately 4 inches apart.

DEPTH: At soil line of seedlings, or just below soil line for sets.

HARVEST TIME: Throughout the season as needed.

Early onions are scallion size, later full grown.

HOW TO GROW GLOBE ONIONS: As soon as soil is workable, plant sets or seedlings 2 inches apart, 1 inch deep, in rows 1 foot apart. All onions prefer full sun. Water thoroughly and keep well watered during the season. During the early part of the season, pull every other plant and use as scallions. When the tops dry in the fall, dig the onions, use them, or slice or mince them in your food processor and freeze.

GARDENER'S TIP 1

Be sure to pick the flower-bearing stalks at the base during the growing season.

PESTS: All onions are quite pest-free.

VARIETY: Southport Globe is one of the best.

COOKING TIP 1

Peel and slice 2 pounds of vine-ripened tomatoes and place them in a bowl. Grate 2 sweet onions and mix them with the tomatoes. Place the bowl in the freezer until the mixture just begins to form ice crystals. Remove it, add an oil and vinegar dressing, and serve immediately. During the hot summer months, this near-iced salad is very refreshing.

EGYPTIAN ONIONS
(WALKING ONIONS)

Egyptian or walking onions are small onion bulbs, which produce bulbils on top of the green stalks instead of flowers. When the top falls, the bulbils plant themselves. Plant them in full sun where they will remain undisturbed by annual Rototilling. The advantage of growing these onions is that they can be harvested very early in the spring. Keep in mind that when you dig them, leave several in the ground so that they can re-sow themselves.

HARDINESS: Annual, very hardy.

WHEN TO PLANT: From early spring to late fall.

SPACING: In a bed, 6 inches apart in all directions.

DEPTH: Just below the soil's surface.

HARVEST TIME: Throughout the season as needed.

HOW TO GROW EGYPTIAN ONIONS: Plant sets or bulbils in a section of the garden that will remain undisturbed. Set them about 6 inches apart, just below the soil line.

GARDENER'S TIP 1

These onions are virtually infallible. Plant them in beds rather than rows. Although not a gardener's primary source of onions, they come in very handy early in the season for flavoring sauces or soups before your other onions are ready to dig.

PESTS: Egyptian onions are pest-free.

VARIETIES: Egyptian or Walking Onions.

Peas

(Pisum sativum)

Petits Pois

These are the tiny little beebee peas favored by the French. There is no trick to growing these vegetables. If you've grown domestic varieties, you can grow these, as cultivation is exactly the same. The secret is knowing when to harvest.

HARDINESS: Annual, tender.

WHEN TO PLANT: In early spring, when ground is workable.

SPACING: Double rows about 1 foot apart. Allow a 2-foot-separation between every three rows for better ventilation. Plant fifteen seeds per foot.

DEPTH: 1 inch.

HARVEST TIME: 6 to 7 weeks.

HOW TO GROW PETITS POIS: Peas are an early crop, suffering in the heat and drought of summer, so you must plant them early. Late March to early April is probably the best time. They like full sun and fairly rich soil in order to produce abundantly. Before you plant the seed, work in compost, rotted manure, and some 5-10-5 fertilizer or organic mixture. Then place 1 inch of unfortified soil on the bottom of a 3-inch-deep row. Plant the seeds fifteen per foot. Cover with 1 to 2 inches of soil and tamp down. The French petits pois grow about 16 inches high, so some support will be necessary for your plants. You can place 2-foot-high twigs in the soil along the row, or build a support with stakes and 3-foot-high chicken wire. After harvesting, simply pull up the stakes and roll up the wire and save it for the following year.

When your plants are about 6 to 8 inches high, sprinkle some 5-10-5 fertilizer or organic mixture lightly on either side of the rows. But make sure you do not overdo it, for peas, being legumes, extract nitrogen from the air. Take care not to allow the granules of fertilizer or organic mixture to come in contact with the leaves of the plant. Keep well cultivated to prevent weeds.

GARDENER'S TIP 1

The secret to delectable petits pois is to pick them when they are very young. I've found the best way to determine when they are ready is to pick one, open it up, and eat the sugar-sweet morsels. If they taste good that way, they'll taste even better on the table.

GARDENER'S TIP 2

Rabbits and birds feast on peas, so enclose your garden with fence. If birds attack as the pods develop, net your pea patch.

GARDENER'S TIP 3

Inoculate your peas before planting. Purchase legume inoculant from a garden center, moisten the seed, pour on the powder, roll the seed in the powder, coating it generously, and plant the seed. Your germination success and yield will be greater.

GARDENER'S TIP 4

After the vines have spent, do not pull them out, but cut them off at the base. The roots add nitrogen and other nutrients to the soil.

PESTS: Pea weevils are brown with gray, black, and white markings and are 1/5 inch long. They damage blossoms and lay egg clusters on young pods. To control use a 57 percent Malathion EC solution (2 tablespoons to 1 gallon of water) and spray the plants while they blossom and before the first pods form. Stop spraying 7 days before harvest. Seed maggots sometimes burrow into seeds, damaging the emerging young plants. You can use Diazinon WP (1 tablespoon to 1 gallon of water) and drench the seed furrows before planting. Wood ashes mixed into the soil before planting are thought to also help to ward off these pests.

VARIETIES: The choice is limited, but both offerings are superb. Petit Provencal is early and very productive. A new variety, Fabina, is a gourmet treat as well. Both freeze well.

Cooking Tip 1

Steam the peas for several minutes, serve with melted butter, and enjoy them. God forbid, don't make a cream sauce for them. As with most Epicurean vegetables, they are at their best served plain with butter.

Snow Peas

These are the edible pea pods ubiquitous in Chinese cuisine. They can be mixed with other ingredients in the preparation of classic dishes or can be stir-fried and eaten alone. Snow peas are rarely available fresh in the markets, and the frozen product is not only expensive but a pale comparison to these sweet fresh morsels.

HARDINESS: Annual, very hardy.

WHEN TO PLANT: In early spring, when ground is workable.

SPACING: In rows about 2 feet apart. Plant seeds 3 inches apart.

DEPTH: 1 to 2 inches.

HARVEST TIME: 6 to 7 weeks.

HOW TO GROW SNOW PEAS: Like petits pois, snow peas are an early crop, averse to the heat and dry spells of summer, so plant as soon as the ground is workable. Full sun and rich soil will produce the best crop, so fortify the soil with compost, rotted manure, and 5-10-5 fertilizer or organic mixture. Plant the seeds about 3 inches apart and cover with 1 to 2 inches of soil. Tamp down and water thoroughly.

Snow peas can grow to a height of 6 to 7 feet if conditions are right, so be sure to provide support. I have found the easiest solution to supporting the vines is to tack plastic netting against posts which I have hammered into the ground. A minimum height of 5 feet is recommended.

As the plants grow, keep them well watered and cultivate to prevent weed growth. When the plants are about 1 foot high, sprinkle 5-10-5 fertilizer or organic mixture on either side of them.

GARDENER'S TIP 1

After 6 weeks, sample some of your snow peas. They should be flat, about 3 to 4 inches long, and they should taste as sweet as sugar. Do not let them grow too large or "fill out," as the pods will be tough and stringy in texture and quite bitter. If they do, shell and use like ordinary peas.

GARDENER'S TIP 2

As with other peas, take precautions against rabbits. Fence is recommended. Plastic netting should protect against birds.

GARDENER'S TIP 3

Inoculating the seeds before planting will ensure good plant growth and high yield in new planting areas. Purchase some inoculant at your garden center, moisten the seeds, pour on the powder, roll the seeds in it, and plant.

GARDENER'S TIP 4

As with petits pois and other peas, do not pull the vines out by the roots when they have spent, but cut them off at the base. The nodules of nitrogen contained will fortify the soil.

GARDENER'S TIP 5

At the end of the bearing season, around the end of June, permit a portion of your crop to "fill out." Do not eat them, but dry them to use the following year when you plant your crop.

PESTS: Pea weevils are brown with gray, black, and white markings and are 1/5 inch long. They damage blossoms and lay egg clusters on young pods. Use a 57 percent Malathion EC solution (2 tablespoons to 1 gallon of water) and spray the plants while they blossom and before the first pods form. Stop spraying 7 days before harvest. Seed maggots sometimes burrow into seeds, damaging the emerging young plants. If you have this problem, take precautions the following year. Use Diazinon WP (1 tablespoon to 1 gallon water) and drench the seed furrows before planting.

VARIETIES: Snow Peas.

COOKING TIP 1

Pick your snow peas just before you are ready to cook them. Many classic Chinese dishes include snow peas. Seafood kow, fu yung chicken, and the superb filet mignon kow are examples. See any basic Chinese cookbook for a recipe using snow peas.

SUGAR SNAPS

Truly a triumph, these superb edible-podded peas were developed in this country. I have seen them for sale in Manhattan's most elegant food emporiums for as much as seven dollars a pint. Ridiculous! If you've grown regular peas, you can grow these. Cultivation and yield are the same. And do believe the glowing reports you read in the seed catalogs about these vegetables. They are everything they say and more. They are a cross between the Oriental snow pea and the conventional pea, with sugar sweet pods and full firm peas inside. You don't shell them, but simply cut them up, pod and all, and cook the entire vegetable or eat them raw in salads. Sugar peas are a bit more rounded in the pod than the flat snow peas when they are ready to eat, and may be eaten semi-mature.

HARDINESS: Annual, very hardy.

WHEN TO PLANT: In early spring, when ground is workable.

SPACING: Rows 2-1/2 feet to 3 feet apart. Plant seeds 1 to 2 inches apart.

DEPTH: 1 to 2 inches.

HARVEST TIME: About 10 weeks.

HOW TO GROW SUGAR SNAP PEAS: Plant as early as soil is workable. As with other peas, full sun and reasonable soil will produce a bumper crop. Fortify the soil with compost, rotted manure, and some 5-10-5 fertilizer or organic mixture. Sow seeds 1 to 2 inches of fine soil. Tamp down and keep moist. The seeds should germinate in 7 to 10 days.

Sugar peas are vigorous growers and can attain a height of 6 feet, so you must provide support. See snow pea cultivation for plastic netting and stake technique.

GARDENER'S TIP 1

Be sure to pick these vegetables when they are young. The pod should be filled out but still tender. The taste test is the best way to ascertain whether or not they are ready to eat.

GARDENER'S TIP 2

As with other peas, rabbits and birds may present problems. Fence your crop to ward off rabbits and net the peas to deter the birds.

GARDENER'S TIP 3

As with other peas, do not pull vines out when spent. Cut off at base and let the roots add nitrogen to the soil.

GARDENER'S TIP 4

Inoculate your seeds before planting to ensure good plant growth and high yield in new planting areas. Purchase inoculant at your local garden center, moisten the seeds, pour on the powder, roll the seed in the powder, and plant.

PESTS: Pea weevils are brown with gray, black, and white markings and are 1/5 inch long. They damage blossoms and lay egg clusters on young pods. Use a 57 percent Malathion EC solution (2 tablespoons to 1 gallon of water) and spray the plants while they blossom and before the first pods form. Stop spraying 7 days before harvest. Seed maggots sometimes burrow into seeds, damaging the emerging young plants. Use Diazinon WP (1 tablespoon to 1 gallon of water) and drench the seed furrows before planting.

VARIETIES: Sugar Snap, Cascadia, standard sized plants growing to from 6-8 feet on a trellis, and Sugar Bon, a dwarf variety, which only grows to about 3 feet. Provide a fence for the dwarf variety.

COOKING TIP 1

Steam this vegetable and serve it with butter or stir-fry. You can also serve it cold and raw in a salad or with a dip.

PEPPERS, HOT

(Capsicum anuum)

CAYENNE CHILI PEPPERS

Cayenne pepper is made from these chili peppers and, like paprika, is hotter and more flavorful when fresh. In order to make your own, all you must do is raise the pepper plant according to instruction and follow the instructions in the "Cooking Tip" section of this entry. It is no more difficult to grow cayenne chili peppers than the sweet bell peppers you probably grow now. The red cayenne pepper grows to about 5 inches long and 1/2 inch thick and is often curled and twisted. It is very hot.

HARDINESS: Annual, tender.

WHEN TO PLANT: Start seeds indoors 6 to 8 weeks before all danger of frost is past. Set outside from mid-May to early June.

SPACING: Indoors: Sow 1 inch apart; outdoors: Plant seedlings 2 feet apart.

DEPTH: Indoors: 1/2 inch; outdoors: Plant seedlings about 1/2 to 1 inch deeper than soil line of seedlings.

HARVEST TIME: In July or August, when peppers are red and ripe.

HOW TO GROW RED CAYENNE CHILI PEPPERS: Start seed indoors in flats filled with a mixture of sand, peat moss, and vermiculite. Sow about 6 to 8 weeks before setting plants out in permanent position in the garden in mid-May or early June, when danger of frost is over. Plant them about 1/2 inch deep, 1 inch apart, water the planting medium thoroughly, and place them in a warm place, about 70 to 80 degrees.

About 1 week later, the seeds will have germinated. Place the flat next to a sunny window, southern exposure preferred. If you have Gro-Lux or fluorescent lights, place the plants under them for about 12 to 14 hours a day.

About a week before outdoor planting time, begin to harden off your plants. Place them outside in the sunshine for a few days and bring them in at night. After they have spent several days outdoors, you can leave them out overnight as long as the temperatures are not too cold, that is below 50 degrees or so.

When all danger of frost is over, and when the seedlings are big enough to handle, plant them 24 inches apart in a sunny spot with well-drained fertile soil. All peppers like a light, friable soil without too much nitrogen. If there is an excess of this element, the plants will go to leaf with little vegetable production. Transplant them on a cloudy day if possible, to avoid wilting from strong sun. Water thoroughly when planting and throughout the growing season.

The problem of cutworm, if truly it is a problem, is included here, rather than in the pest section, as a simple precaution at planting time will save your pepper plants from the ravages of this pest. Cutworms eat the tender stems of peppers, tomatoes, and eggplant. In a single night, they can level your entire planting of young peppers. Simply fashion a collar out of cardboard, aluminum foil, or tin cans and insert it about 1 inch below soil level to about 3 inches above soil level. This will protect your plant.

By July, your pepper plants will produce small fruits which will slowly turn brilliant red. When they are red and ripe, pick them and prepare for drying.

GARDENER'S TIP 1

Pepper plants are attractive; if space is at a premium, work them into your flower garden or border.

PESTS: If blossom-end rot attacks your plants, dark, sunken leathery spots will appear on the blossom end of the fruit. This problem is likely to occur after dry spells during early growth. Regular watering will probably spare you this outrage.

VARIETY: Long Red Cayenne Pepper.

COOKING TIP 1

To make dried cayenne chili peppers, use only the "walls" of the peppers. Seeds, tissue, and stems are not suitable. Place the "walls" on a screen in a warm, shady, dry place and allow them to dry out. Or dry them in a slow oven (150 degrees) until brittle. When they are bone dry, grind them with a food processor or by hand with a mortar and pestle. Store in glass jar or other moisture-proof container in the refrigerator. For spanking fresh cayenne pepper, place the brittle "walls" in the refrigerator and grind the spice as needed.

J A L A P E Ñ O S   A N D   O T H E R   H O T   C H I L I   P E P P E R S

SEE CAYENNE PEPPERS. CULTIVATION IS THE SAME.

There are many varieties of hot peppers, ranging from mild to
  super hot. Here are some:

Paper Dragon, medium hot, large.

Flash, medium hot, slender.

Thai Dragon, small pointed, very hot.

Super Chili, very small and hot.

Ortega, long thick mildly hot.

Ancho, medium hot heart shaped.

Mulato Isleno, chocolate brown sweet flesh, hot pith.

Sugar Chile, very sweet, medium long, tapered, pointed fruit. Good
  for roasting.

Giant Jalapeño, medium hot, thick flesh, the biggest true Jalapeño.

Delicias, mild, large.

Pretty in Purple, beautifully ornamental with purple foliage and
  small 3/4 inch round glossy peppers in deep purple which ripen
  yellow orange and finally scarlet. Spectacular to look at.

Cherry Bomb, round fruit, hot.

P A P R I K A   O R   H U N G A R I A N   W A X   P E P P E R S

Paprika is the Hungarian word for red pepper. And spanking-fresh paprika is difficult to obtain unless you happen to be fortunate enough to live near a purveyor who imports the spice from Hungary. But with no more effort than it takes to grow domestic peppers, you can grow the variety used to produce fresh paprika. Making your own is simply a matter of growing the vegetable properly, drying the fruits, and grinding them to powder consistency.

HARDINESS: Annual, tender.

WHEN TO PLANT: Start seeds indoors 6 to 8 weeks before all danger of frost is past. Set outside mid-May to early June.

SPACING: Indoors: Sow 1 inch apart; outdoors: plant seedlings 2 feet apart.

DEPTH: Indoors:1/2 inch; outdoors: Just below the soil line of seedling.

HARVEST TIME: Pick in July when peppers are red and ripe.

HOW TO GROW HUNGARIAN WAX PEPPERS: Start the seeds indoors in flats filled with a mixture of sand, peat moss, and vermiculite. Plan on sowing about 6 to 8 weeks before setting plants out in mid-May or early June. Sow about 1/2 inch deep, 1 inch apart, water thoroughly, and place in a warm area, about 70 to 80 degrees.

In approximately 1 week, when the seeds have germinated and small leaves appear, place the plants next to a sunny window (southern exposure preferred). Or place them under fluorescent lights for about 12 to 14 hours a day.

About 2 weeks before planting time, harden off the plants by placing them outdoors during the daylight hours.

After all danger of frost is past, plant your pepper plants about 2 feet apart in a sunny, well-drained, fertile spot. Peppers prefer light, friable soil, not too rich in nitrogen. Too much nitrogen forces the plants to go to leaf with sparse vegetable production. Transplant on a cloudy day in order to avoid wilting problems. Water thoroughly at planting time and throughout the summer.

Be advised that cutworms can be a problem with peppers. Simply fashion a collar of cardboard or other material at the base of the plant and sink it into the ground about 1 inch.

By July, the pepper plants will produce small, yellow-green fruits which will gradually turn brilliant red as they ripen. When ripe and red, pick them and prepare for drying.

GARDENER'S TIP 1

Peppers are almost pest-free; however, blossom-end rot may attack your plants. Apply non hazardous doses of lime and super-phosphate to counter a calcium deficiency. This problem is likely to occur after dry spells during the early part of the season. Conscientious watering will help you to avoid this problem.

PESTS: Occasionally, climbing cutworms can eat at the stems of plants, killing them. To control this fashion paper cylinder collars and place them around the bottom of the plant. In this way cutworms cannot get to the main stem and climb up to eat. It is best to water using an irrigation hose, as peppers can get bacterial spot from wet foliage.

VARIETY: Hungarian Wax Pepper.

COOKING TIP 1

Hungarian Wax Pepper, which has a long, slender, pointed pod about 4 or 5 inches long, will produce a mild and mellow-flavored spice with a rich, red color. Use only the "walls" of the peppers. Discard the seeds, tissue, and stems. Place the "walls" on a screen in a warm, shady, dry place and let them dry out. Or dry them in a slow oven (150 degrees) until brittle. When the peppers are bone dry, grind them with a food processor or by hand with a mortar and pestle. Store in glass jars or other moisture proof containers in the refrigerator. For the freshest spice, save the brittle "walls" and grind the spice as needed.

COOKING TIP 2

Of course paprika is an essential ingredient in one of the world's great cuisines, that of Hungary. A delicious mushroom dish is easily prepared by sautéing 1 pound fresh mushrooms in 2 tablespoons butter and 1 teaspoon fresh lemon juice. After about 5 minutes, add 2 tablespoons minced onion, 1 teaspoon flour, 2 teaspoons paprika, 1/2 teaspoon salt, and a dash of cayenne pepper. Mix the ingredients and add 1/3 cup sour cream. Heat, but don't boil. Serve hot.

TABASCO CHILI PEPPERS

If you decide to grow these peppers, not only can you use them in cooking, but you can make your own Tabasco sauce out of them. They are extremely hot in taste.

HARDINESS: Annual, tender.

WHEN TO PLANT: Start seeds indoors 6 to 8 weeks before all danger of frost is over. Set outside mid-May to early June.

SPACING: Indoors: Sow seeds 1 inch apart; outdoors: Plant seedlings 2 feet apart.

DEPTH: Indoors: 1/2 inch; outdoors: About 1/2 inch deeper than soil line of seedlings.

HARVEST TIME: In July or August when chili peppers are red and ripe.

HOW TO GROW TABASCO CHILI PEPPERS: Start seed indoors in flats filled with a mixture of sand, peat moss, and vermiculite. Sow about 6 to 8 weeks before setting out in mid-May or early June when danger of frost is over. Plant about 1/2 inch deep, 1 inch apart, water the planting medium thoroughly, and place flats in a warm place, about 70 to 80 degrees.

About a week later the seeds will have germinated. Place the flat in a sunny window, southern exposure preferred. If you have Gro-Lux or fluorescent lights, place the plants under them for about 12 to 14 hours a day.

About a week before outdoor planting time, begin to harden your plants off. Place them outside in the sunshine for a few days and bring them in at night. After they have spent several days outdoors you can leave them out overnight as long as the nights are not cold.

When all danger of frost is over, or in early June when the seedlings are big enough to handle, plant them 2 feet apart in a sunny, well-drained, fertile spot. All peppers like friable, light soil with not too much nitrogen content. If there is an excess of this element, the plants will go to leaf with little vegetable production. Transplant your seedlings on a cloudy day if possible to avoid the sun's strong rays. Water thoroughly when planting and then throughout the summer.

Be sure to fashion collars for these plants, as cutworms may attack them. Simply encircle the plant with aluminum foil which you have sunk into the soil to a depth of about 1 inch. By August, the chili pepper plants will produce small fruits which will turn brilliant red. When they are red and ripe, pick them and either use them for cooking or make Tabasco sauce out of them.

GARDENER'S TIP 1

Tabasco chili pepper plants are attractive and can be worked into your flower bed or border.

PESTS: Regular watering during dry spells will help counter blossom-end rot.

VARIETY: Tabasco.

COOKING TIP 1

To make your own Tabasco sauce, pick and wash chili peppers. Cut into pieces and discard stems, seeds, and white pithy interior. To make about 1 pint of Tabasco sauce, you will need about 2 quarts of pepper "walls." Place peppers in 2-quart pot. Add about 3/4 pint of white vinegar and 4 cloves minced garlic. Cover with lid. Simmer slowly for about 1-1/2 hours. Taste to see if your Tabasco sauce is hot enough. If it isn't, steep for 1/2 hour. Add additional vinegar if necessary. Strain, put in jar, and store in a cool, dry place. You can use your Tabasco sauce immediately. It will keep indefinitely.

PEPPERS, SWEET

(Capsicum anuum)

Sweet Peppers are grown in exactly the same way that hot peppers are. Pests and diseases are the same, culture is the same. So simply follow instructions for hot peppers above. Since they are so spectacularly attractive, sweet peppers have become an important part of today's cuisine. And beyond their healthful qualities, they are beautiful to look at. There are so many different kinds of sweet peppers in a rainbow of colors. Here are some: Green Ripening Red: Ace, King Arthur, Vanguard, Northstar, Lantern; Orange: Corona Valencia; Chocolate: Sweet Chocolate; Purple: Lavender, Islander, Secret.

RADICCHIO

(Chicorium endiva)

Virtually unknown in the United States until about 15 years ago, this favorite Italian member of the chicory family is now one of the status vegetables, its deep red color and bitter sweet flavor adding so much to the salad bowl. It's not difficult to grow, as long as you are aware that the plant must be cut back and re-grown before you can harvest it.

HARDINESS: Annual, hardy.

WHEN TO PLANT: Plant varieties which must be cut back in mid to late May and varieties which do not have to be cut back in mid spring, when ground is workable.

SPACING: Plant in rows 2 feet apart, thin to 1 foot apart.

DEPTH: 1/4 inch.

HARVEST TIME: Late summer for varieties which do not have to be cut back. Mid to late fall for varieties that have to be cut back.

HOW TO GROW RADICCHIO: In most parts of the United States, plant seeds in the ground during late May or early June, then around Labor Day, cut plants back. They will re-sprout and be ready for harvest 4-6 weeks later. There are two varieties which do not need to be cut back. These are Castlefranco and Giulio. Both produce harvestable heads in from 80-85 days.

VARIETIES: Early Treviso is a fast grower. You can plant in mid July and cut back on Labor day for a fall crop. Red Verona, the most popular, produces bright red heads the size of a baseball with prominent white veins and an intriguingly bitter flavor. Castlefranco has marbled red and white coloring and its heads do not have to be cut back. Giulio can be planted successively throughout the summer. It has deep burgundy heads with white veins and need not be cut back.

RADISHES

For the most part, radishes in the United States are nothing more than red, wooden marbles, packed in plastic and used as garnish to add color to platters of other vegetables or to salads. In the Far East, radishes are eaten as frequently and with as much gusto as are potatoes in this country. And they are prepared in many different ways: steamed, boiled, stir-fried, pickled, and deep-fried.

DAIKON

HARDINESS: Annual, very hardy.

WHEN TO PLANT: In early spring, when ground is workable.

SPACING: In rows 1 foot apart. Sow seeds thinly and thin out to 4 inches apart.

DEPTH: About 1/2 inch.

HARVEST TIME: In fall.

HOW TO GROW DAIKON: Plant as soon as the ground is workable and then again at 2-week intervals throughout the season until early fall. Place your bed in full sun, and fortify the soil with a good sprinkling of 5-10-5 fertilizer or organic mixture. Sow the seeds thinly about 1/2 inch deep and when seedlings are about 1 inch thin to 4 inches apart. (Keep in mind that Daikon radishes come in many shapes and sizes, so be sure to check your seed package for thinning instructions.)

For small, young Daikon, harvest in about 4 weeks. For fully mature specimens, harvest in about 2 months. Again, check package instructions for harvest time with individual varieties.

PESTS: If you have had trouble with root maggots tunneling through your domestic radishes, chances are you will have the same problem with Oriental varieties. Apply Diazinon crystals according to instructions on the package. Wood ashes worked into the soil may possibly help ward off these pests.

VARIETIES: Spring Song, Summer Cross No. 3, Miyashige.

COOKING TIP 1

Daikon is very versatile. To prepare for cooking, peel and cut as you would carrots. The most obvious way to prepare them is to stir-fry or steam and serve with your favorite Oriental condiments. But the Japanese shred 1/2 pound Daikon and 1/2 pound carrots, soak them in cold water for 30 minutes, drain, and then combine them with a salad dressing made of 1 cup vinegar, 1/2 cup sugar, 1 teaspoon salt, and 1/2 teaspoon monosodium glutamate. All ingredients are heated just until the sugar dissolves. Use only enough to moisten the shredded vegetables. The rest stores well in the refrigerator.

FRENCH BREAKFAST RADISHES

These are probably the mildest, sweetest radishes grown. As with all radishes, there's nothing to growing them. They're small, about half the size of an adult's pinky, and believe it or not, a treat even at breakfast time.

HARDINESS: Annual, very hardy.

WHEN TO PLANT: In early spring, as soon as ground is workable. Successive plantings every 7 days until the heat of summer, and then again in the fall.

SPACING: Rows about 1 foot apart; plant seeds 1/2 inch apart and thin to 1 inch.

DEPTH: 3/4 inch.

HARVEST TIME: 18 days.

HOW TO GROW FRENCH BREAKFAST RADISHES: Plant as soon as the ground is workable and then again at 7-day intervals throughout the spring. The secret of producing mild and sweet radishes is quick growth, so accommodate them with the proper growing conditions: that is, full sun, a good dose of water at least once a week, and an initial fortification of the soil with sprinklings of 5-10-5 fertilizer or organic mixture. Sow the seeds 3/4 inch deep, about 1/2 inch apart, and thin to 1 inch when seedlings are about 1 inch high. Harvest in 18 days.

GARDENER'S TIP 1

If you find when you dig your radishes that they have split, they are too old. Dispose of them.

PESTS: Plant a trial run to see if root maggots tunnel into your crop. If so, when you plant your subsequent crops, apply Diazinon crystals as directed on the package. Wood ashes are sometimes thought to help alleviate this problem. Other than this pest, radishes are pest-free.

VARIETY: 18-Day Radish.

COOKING TIP 1

Try these just with sweet butter and a little salt and pepper. That is how the French eat them.

Rhubarb

(Rheum x cultorum)

After initial planting, rhubarb is virtually maintenance-free, all the more reason to set in several plants. A bountiful supply of this delicious vegetable-fruit will be yours all spring long and well into the summer. Unfortunately, rhubarb is not adapted to most parts of the South, though in certain areas of higher elevation it does grow fairly well. Check locally to be sure your area is appropriate for growing. A few plants along the garden fence will supply all that a family can use.

HARDINESS: Perennial, hardy.

WHEN TO PLANT: In early spring, when ground is workable.

SPACING: 3 to 4 feet apart.

DEPTH: Soil line of plant.

HARVEST TIME: 2 to 3 years after planting, in early to late spring in particular, but all seasons in moderation, if desired.

HOW TO GROW RHUBARB: Any deep, well-drained, fertile soil in full sun is suitable for rhubarb. Spade the soil or plow it to a depth of 12 to 16 inches and mix in rotted manure, leaf mold, compost, or other form of organic matter. Since rhubarb is planted in hills 3 to 4 feet apart, it is generally sufficient to prepare each hill separately.

The best way to start your rhubarb is to purchase plants in the early spring. Most garden centers have a supply of this plant, but if not, you can order from almost any mail order nursery.

Set the plants out at soil level. You can easily see this by looking at the stem of your specimen. The plant you buy was grown in soil, so just set it at the same level. Each year, in either spring or fall, top-dress the planting with a heavy application of rotted manure, compost, or 10-6-4 commercial fertilizer. About 1 pound of this per hill will suffice.

At some point during the season, a large bulbous seed bud will develop at the tip of each plant. Remove these immediately, for if left to develop, they will divert valuable nutrients from the edible stalks.

Every seven or eight years the plants will become too thick and will produce only slender edible stems. Dig these in the fall, split the roots into sections having at least two to three buds as well as a heavy root system, and replant in a different section of the garden. Each division will develop into a new plant.

Do not pick any stems the first year. Pick sparingly the second year, and then as much as you like after that. To pick rhubarb, remove the stem by gripping it near the base and pulling and twisting to one side. The stalk will break easily from the plant. Do not pick any more than one-third of the stems during any given year.

GARDENER'S TIP 1

Remove all leaves from the stems after you have picked them. Do not under any circumstances use them for food, as they contain poisonous substances, including oxalic acid.

PESTS: There are none.

VARIETIES: Canada Red, Crimson, MacDonald, Red Valentine, and Victoria are all standard varieties.

COOKING TIP 1

Of course, rhubarb pie is delicious, but a strawberry-rhubarb pie is even better. Simply add one or two cups (depending on how much you like rhubarb) of 1 to 1-1/2 inch pieces of peeled rhubarb to the strawberries when you fill the pie crust. And yes, it is something to write home about.

SHALLOTS

(Allium ascalonicium)

The highly praised member of the onion family, the shallot (pronounced with the accent on the final syllable, incidentally) resembles a small tulip bulb, with a shiny brown skin which when peeled reveals a purple outer surface. The taste of the shallot clove lies somewhere between an onion and garlic and is highly esteemed in classic French and northern Italian cuisine when a distinctive onion taste is desired.

HARDINESS: Annual, very hardy.

WHEN TO PLANT: In early spring, when ground is workable.

SPACING: Rows 1 foot apart, plant sets 6 inches apart.

DEPTH: With pointed tops just below soil surface.

HARVEST TIME: Late August, early September.

HOW TO GROW SHALLOTS: Anyone who has grown onions can grow shallots. Culture and requirements are exactly the same. Order your shallot sets from a mail order seed house, or if they are available in your supermarket or a specialty store, you can plant those. Shallots like a light, friable, well-drained soil with lots of humus or compost worked into it to ensure a constant source of nutrients for a heavy yield. If your sets consist of an entire bulb like a garlic, which you might buy in the market, separate each bulb into individual cloves. Place them in the ground in full sun, about 4 inches apart with the blunt end down. Cover them with soil so that the pointed tops are just below the level of the garden soil. Once planted, water them well. In about 10 days or so, they will begin to grow.

During the season, keep the soil around your shallots well cultivated. Weed competition will dwarf your harvest at the end of the season. During drought, water thoroughly.

Wait until late August or early September to harvest. When the leaves have turned brown and have almost died down, dig the shallots and place them on a screen in the sun to dry. Provide adequate ventilation during the drying period. The following week, cut off the tops, rub the dead leaves, skin, and dry soil off, and store the bulbs in a cool, dry place. Each shallot bulb will produce a cluster of six or more cloves.

GARDENER'S TIP 1

Some people have success planting shallots in the fall, wintering the mover, and harvesting them early in the summer. I have not tried this method, as the spring planting has always been quite successful for me.

GARDENER'S TIP 2

Be sure to save enough shallots from your fall crop for the following years planting.

GARDENER'S TIP 3

Shallots are among the easiest of all vegetables to grow.

PESTS: Few, if any.

VARIETIES: Atlas, Ambition, Eds Red, Creation.

COOKING TIP 1

Check your cookbooks for recipes calling for shallots. For convenience, shallots can be chopped or minced in the food processor, frozen as is, and then used as needed. This will save you time mincing or chopping each time they are called for in a recipe.

COOKING TIP 2

If you find winter supermarket onions are too strong for some of your creations, simply substitute shallots for a milder taste. A superb salad dressing can be made with essence of shallot. To make the essence, boil 1 cup white wine. Add 4 tablespoons chopped shallots and boil for 5 minutes. Strain and combine with olive or walnut oil for a dressing your garden-grown greens deserve.

SORREL

This is the delightful tart green leaf which the French use to make potage germiny. Middle and Eastern European Christians and Jews have known sorrel well for centuries as sourgrass soup and Schav. Problem is when you encounter a recipe which says, "First take one pound of fresh sorrel . . . etc.," where on earth do you go to buy it? Growing your own is so simple there's no need to deprive yourself of this very special treat.

HARDINESS: Perennial, very hardy.

WHEN TO PLANT: In early spring, when ground is workable.

SPACING: In rows 1 foot apart, sow thinly and thin to 1 foot apart.

DEPTH: 1/2 inch.

HARVEST TIME: 8 weeks after planting first year, then throughout the season in subsequent years.

HOW TO GROW SORREL: Select a site in your garden that will remain undisturbed. Sorrel is perennial, so you will want to plant out of the way of the annual Rototilling. If possible plant in a semishaded spot, as full sunlight tends to toughen the leaves somewhat.

Sorrel likes a rich loam, so fortify your soil with compost, rotted manure, bonemeal, and some 5-10-5 fertilizer or organic mixture. Dig in to a depth of about 1 foot. Each fall renew the soil with a top dressing of nutrients or fertilizer.

Sow seeds 1/2 inch deep in rows 1 foot apart. When the seedlings are about 1 inch high, thin them out to 6 inches apart. Then in the fall, when they have reached maturity, thin them to 1 foot apart.

Gardener's Tip 1

During the summer, flowering shoots will grow from the plant. As soon as they appear, cut them off, as they rob the plants of nourishment and prevent leaves from reaching maximum size.

Gardener's Tip 2

After your sorrel patch is established, pick leaves from the outside of the clump. This will permit the plant to spread vigorously.

Gardener's Tip 3

Rabbits relish sorrel, so provide fence to ward them off.

PESTS: There are none.

VARIETY: French Sorrel.

Cooking Tip 1

Because of its piquant lemony taste, shredded sorrel is the perfect accompaniment to fish dishes. Simply shred the leaves, gently sauté them in butter until limp then use them in a fish sauce or simply poured over the fish. The lemony taste is wonderful.

Squash

(Cucurbita)

PATTY PANS

These are the deep yellow summer squash so favored by today's gourmet. They are appetizing in color and you can pick them when they are tiny, with the blossom still attached, or wait until they are more mature, the size of a teacup.

HARDINESS: Annual, hardy.

WHEN TO PLANT: In spring, after all danger of frost. The same time that tomatoes are planted in your area.

SPACING: Plant 2-3 seeds every 9-12 inches and thin to one plant per foot.

DEPTH: 1/2 to 1 inch.

HARVEST TIME: Early summer to early fall.

HOW TO GROW PATTY PAN SQUASH: Plant in full sun or partial shade in soil which has been fortified with rotted compost or manure, or a sprinkling of 5-10-5 fertilizer, at the rate of about 1 tablespoon per square foot.

GARDENER'S TIP 1

If you sow seeds before the last frost date in your area, cold soil will rot the seeds.

PESTS: Cucumber beetles can carry bacterial wilt and must be controlled. Check with your local cooperative extension to find out which fungicide is recommended in your area. Insects which may attack are squash bugs, cucumber beetles and vine borers. Rotenone and pyrethrum offer some control. A clean and tidy garden is a great help in keeping down pest invasion.

VARIETIES: Sunburst, Bennings, Green Tint.

COOKING TIP 1

Pick these when they are quite small (when the blossom is still attached to the vegetable) and serve them individually as a side vegetable.

SPAGHETTI SQUASH

Spaghetti squash is another of the recent additions to the gourmet vegetable scene in the United States. It has only been in the last year or so that seeds for this vegetable have been available in seed racks at your local garden center. Cultivation is the same for other summer squash such as zucchini and yellow squash. When this vegetable is cooked, the flesh separates into spaghetti-like strands with a slightly crunchy texture. It is, to say the least, very good to eat and, if you are weight-conscious, very low in calories.

HARDINESS: Annual, hardy.

WHEN TO PLANT: In spring, after all danger of frost. The same time that tomatoes are planted in your area.

SPACING: In hills 4 to 6 feet apart, two to four plants per hill.

DEPTH: 1/2 inch.

HARVEST TIME: About 90 to 100 days.

HOW TO GROW SPAGHETTI SQUASH: Plant your spaghetti squash in full sun after all danger of frost is over. Like cucumbers and melons, squash is planted in small mounds measuring about 1-1/2 feet across, set 4 feet apart. Dig about a shovelful of rotted manure and compost into the hollow of your squash mound. Also mix in about 1 pound of 5-10-5 fertilizer or 2 pounds of organic mixture. Then cover the nutrients with soil. Plant three to five seeds in a circle near the center of the mound and cover with 1/2 inch of soil After the seeds have germinated, remove all but two or three plants per hill. If you have fertilized at planting time, additional fertilizer will not be necessary during the growing season. Keep well watered during dry periods and remove weed growth as it appears.

GARDENER'S TIP 1

Spaghetti squash should be picked when young and tender. Your crop should be ready in about 90 to 100 days. If your fingernail cannot puncture the skin, the squash is too old, so be sure to harvest when the fruits are young. If you permit the squash to remain on the vine until it becomes large and pulpy, the results will be disappointing and your plant will probably not bear much more produce.

GARDENER'S TIP 2

To conserve moisture, keep weeds down, and to ensure warm soil for rapid growth, black plastic laid down on your squash patch will do wonders. After you've prepared your bed, cover the entire area with the synthetic mulch. Then cut holes where you wish to plant the seeds and put them in place.

GARDENER'S TIP 3

I have not had difficulties with rabbits eating spaghetti squash, so I do not cover my crop with chicken wire.

GARDENER'S TIP 4

Spaghetti squash will store well in a cool, dry place.

PESTS: Cucumber beetles can carry bacterial wilt and must be controlled. Check with your local cooperative extension to find out which fungicide is recommended in your area. Insects which may attack are squash bugs, cucumber beetles and vine borers. Rotenone and pyrethrum offer some control. Keeping your garden clean and tidy is one of the best ways to keep this pest invasion down.

VARIETY: Vegetable Spaghetti.

COOKING TIP 1

Spaghetti squash can be prepared as you would any summer squash such as zucchini. Try it with your favorite pesto recipe.

YELLOW CROOKNECKS

Many consider this the finest summer squash for buttery flavor and firm texture. It is a late bearing plant, but once it starts to yield harvesting is consistent over a long period.

HARDINESS: Annual, hardy.

WHEN TO PLANT: In spring, after all danger of frost. The same time that tomatoes are planted in your area.

SPACING: Plant 2-3 seeds ever 9-12 inches and thin to one plant per foot.

DEPTH: 1/2 to 1 inch.

HARVEST TIME: Early summer to early fall.

HOW TO GROW YELLOW CROOKNECK SQUASH: See Pattypan Squash for further growing instructions.

PESTS: Cucumber beetles can carry bacterial wilt and must be controlled. Check with your local cooperative extension to find out which fungicide is recommended in your area. Insects which may attack are squash bugs, cucumber beetles and vine borers. Rotenone and pyrethrum offer some control. A clean and tidy garden is a great help in keeping down pest invasion.

VARIETIES: Yellow Crookneck.

COOKING TIP 1

Pick these when they are only 4-5 inches long, when they have a bulbous shape and a narrow, curved neck. It is best to cook them as soon as possible after picking. Steam them whole till they are tender but still slightly crisp, then drizzle with melted butter and sprinkle with cracked black pepper and parmesan cheese as a delicious side dish. Or slice diagonally and stir fry with bok choy, garlic, and green onions. Toss with soy sauce and serve over rice.

SPROUTS

This is an indoor crop easily grown. The bean sprouts you buy in the supermarket, and other sprouts as well, can be germinated in your own kitchen in about 1 week.

HOW TO GROW SPROUTS

1. PLACE SEEDS IN A JAR. A quart jar works well for about 2 to 3 tablespoons of sprouting seeds. Be sure to select culinary sprouting seeds from the grocery market or health food store. Seeds from a seed nursery or garden store may sometimes have been treated with chemicals to help them resist diseases when planted.

2. MOISTEN. Fill the jar three-fourths full with warm water. Shake the jar vigorously for about 10 to 15 seconds. Drain the water away. Some health food stores sell sprouting jars or sprouting jar lids with plastic mesh tops that are convenient for rinsing the seeds without losing them down the drain. You can also use a layer of cheesecloth held on the jar by the metal ring of a two-part canning jar lid, or by rubber bands.

3. RINSE DAILY WITH COOL WATER. Once or twice each day, pour cool water into the jar to cover seeds and new sprouts, swish gently, and drain. Sprouts are ready to eat in about a week. Refrigerate when the jar is filled with crisp green edible sprouts.

VARIETIES: Alfalfa (especially good on salads), mung beans (especially for Chinese cooking), fenugreek (for a spicy taste).

COOKING TIP 1

Alfalfa sprouts are delightful with cream cheese in little finger sandwiches. Fenugreek sprouts have a delicious spicy flavor with a touch of maple.

COOKING TIP 2

The Chinese stir-fry whole mung bean sprouts for about 1 minutes and add a few drops of sesame oil and vinegar.

TOKYO TURNIPS

(Brassica rapa)

In the Far East, this vegetable is pickled, but I serve it raw in salads or with dips. Tokyo turnips are sweet, tender, pure white, very appetizing, and add a nutty crunchy texture to the crudités tray. They're very easily grown and a delight to the palate.

HARDINESS: Annual, hardy.

WHEN TO PLANT: In early spring, as soon as ground is workable.

SPACING: In rows 1 foot apart, plant seeds 1 inch apart, thinning to 4 inches apart.

DEPTH: 1/2 inch.

HARVEST TIME: In about 30 to 40 days for tender young specimens.

HOW TO GROW TOKYO TURNIPS: In early spring as soon as ground is workable, plant in full sun. Fertilize soil modestly with rotted manure, compost, and a sprinkling of 5-10-5 fertilizer or organic mixture. Keep well watered, cultivate to discourage weeds, and check for harvest in about 30 to 40 days. Pull when young, about 1-1/2 inches in diameter.

GARDENER'S TIP 1

Plant successive crops every 2 weeks until hot weather for a continuous supply, then plant again in the fall for a later crop.

PESTS: Tokyo turnips seem to be pest-free.

VARIETIES: Chung Choy, Tokyo Turnip, Tokyo Cross Hybrid Turnip.

COOKING TIP 1

Tokyo turnips combine particularly well with snow peas when stir-fried. They can also be eaten raw with a dip or sliced in salad. The taste is peppery, akin to a very mild horseradish taste.

TOMATILLOS

(P. ixocarpa)

Tomatillos look like little green tomatoes in paper husks, but they are actually related to the ground cherry, not to tomatoes. Their slightly lemony flavor is the special ingredient in some of the fresh green salsas accompanying authentic Mexican cookery and Southwestern cuisine.

HARDINESS: Annual, tender.

WHEN TO PLANT: Start indoors in flats under lights 4-6 weeks before last frost. Set outside at the same time that you set out tomatoes.

SPACING: 3 feet apart.

DEPTH: Sow seeds in flats 1/4 inch deep. Set outside at level grown in container.

HARVEST TIME: From mid summer to frost.

HOW TO GROW TOMATILLOS: Cultivation is exactly the same as for tomatoes.

GARDENER'S TIP 1

Tomatillos, also called husk tomatoes, offer fruit that is encased in a husk which looks like a Chinese lantern. When the fruit is ripe, the papery husk turns brown. The fruit inside is yellow.

PESTS: Cucumber beetles or Colorado potato beetles may attack. Use Sevin or rotenone organic insecticide according to instructions on the package.

VARIETIES: Toma Verde, fruits grow to golf-ball size, with paper lanterns over them. This variety is the secret ingredient in salsa; Golden Tomatillo and Cape Gooseberry have small, yellow fruits encased in papery husks.

COOKING TIP 1

Here's a classic green salsa recipe that is very popular in Mexico: Heat a heavy dry skillet on the stove and put 6 tomatillos in it (remove the papery husk but don't peel the tomatillos). Toss in 3 or 4 cloves of garlic and about 1/4 peeled onion. Roast over medium heat till these are slightly charred in places and are somewhat softened. Meanwhile put 1 or 2 scrubbed chipotle chiles (the dried smoky ones) or other hot dried chilies in half a cupful of boiling water and allow to soak a bit. Remove the roasted vegetables from the skillet to a food processor or blender and add the strained soaking water from the hot chilies plus 1/2 teaspoon of sea salt. Whirl. Before serving, you can work this through a sieve for smoother salsa, or leave it coarse. Thin with water or more chili soaking water if you like it hot. Add a handful of chopped fresh cilantro if desired.

TOMATOES

(Lycopersicon esculentum)

CHERRY TOMATOES

During the height of the summer season, there is nothing quite like the taste of a massive beefsteak tomato or the spectacular new hybrid varieties of standard tomatoes. But for salads and hors d'oeuvre, these tiny versions make for tidy eating. You can just pick them and put them in your mouth, all in one bite. They are excellent salad and snack material for people on diets. No Epicurean garden should be without at least several of these midget tomato plants.

HARDINESS: Annual, tender.

WHEN TO PLANT: Start seeds indoors 6 to 8 weeks before all danger of frost is past. Set outside mid-May to early June.

SPACING: Indoors: Sow 1 inch apart; outdoors: Plant seedlings about 1 foot apart.

DEPTH: Indoors: 1/2 inch; outdoors: Plant just below first pair of leaves on plant, regardless of soil line.

HARVEST TIME: 55 to 75 days.

HOW TO GROW CHERRY TOMATOES: Start your plants indoors from 6 to 8 weeks before outdoor planting time, mid-May to early June. Fill flats with a mixture of peat moss, sand, and vermiculite. Plant seeds about 1/2 inch deep and 1 inch apart, water the planting medium thoroughly, and place the flat in a warm place, about 70 to 80 degrees.

When the seeds have germinated, in about a week, place the flat in a window that receives full southern sun. If you use GroLux or other fluorescent lights, place the plants under them for about 12 to 14 hours a day. About a week before planting time, harden your plants off. Place them outside during the day and bring them indoors at night. Then several days before planting, leave them out overnight if the nights are not too cold. By the end of that week leave them out overnight. When you transplant, if possible pick an overcast day. Hot sun might wilt your plants. Set the plants out in the garden about 1 foot to 18 inches apart.

As with other tomatoes, peppers, and eggplants, fashion a collar out of tin foil, cardboard or cut-off milk cartons to place around the stem. This will serve to ward off cutworms.

Before you plant, fertilize the ground sparingly with compost, rotted manure, and a sparse handful of 5-10-5 fertilizer or organic mixture. Set your plants in the soil with the lowest pair of leaves at soil level. Set the collar around each plant about 1 inch into the soil and about 3 inches above the soil line.

Stake the plants when they have grown to about 6 inches in height. Drive a 3-foot stake into the ground about 3 inches from the main stem of the plant. As your cherry tomatoes grow, tie them firmly to the stake. Keep your plants weed-free and irrigate profusely during dry spells. All tomatoes require plenty of moisture in order to produce abundantly. Harvest tomatoes as they turn deep red.

GARDENER'S TIP 1

Pinch all suckers that grow from between the leaf stems and the stalk. Let the plant energy form tomatoes instead of leaves.

GARDENER'S TIP 2

Cherry tomatoes adapt nicely to tub planting as well as indoor gardening. For a winter crop, sow seeds outdoors in August in pots. When they attain a height of about 6 inches, bring them indoors to a sunny window. The plants should provide lots of cherry tomatoes throughout the winter.

GARDENER'S TIP 3

If you start these indoors well before planting time, you should have bearing plants by the time you are ready to set them out. In this way, you can have that fresh, vine-ripened-tasting tomato long before the standard tomatoes begin to bear.

PESTS: Tomato hornworm is green with diagonal lines on sides and a prominent spike or horn on the rear. Hand-pick the worms and immerse in kerosene or bleach. If you choose to spray, a 50 percent Sevin WP (2 tablespoons to 1 gallon of water) should be applied when the worms appear. A 5 percent rotenone WP (5 tablespoons to 1 gallon of water) will keep flea beetles under control. These are pin-head-sized, black, brown, or striped jumping beetles about 1/16 inch long.

VARIETIES: There are many. Tiny Tim is the earliest, Cherry Tomato the most popular. Sungold is a yellow variety which have a tropical or winey taste.

COOKING TIP 1

These tiny tomatoes make perfect hors d'oeuvre, as they are bite-size and can be picked up with the fingers. If you grow them in pots indoors in the winter, you won't have to resort to the tasteless variety available in the markets.

ROMA TOMATOES

Sometimes you can find six-packs of this variety of tomato in your local garden center at planting time. To be sure you have planting stock, start seeds 6 to 8 weeks before setting-out time. These tomatoes are the paste-type or plum tomatoes from which Italian sauce is made. Cultivation is exactly the same as for standard tomatoes.

HARDINESS: Annual, tender.

WHEN TO PLANT: Start seeds indoors 6 to 8 weeks before all danger of frost is past. Set outside from mid-May on.

SPACING: Indoors: Sow 1 inch apart; outdoors: Plant seedlings 2 feet apart.

DEPTH: Indoors: 1/2 inch; Outdoors: plant just below first pair of leaves on plant, regardless of soil line.

HARVEST TIME: 72 to 76 days.

HOW TO GROW ROMA TOMATOES Start seeds indoors from 6 to 8 weeks before outdoor planting time after danger of frost is past. Plant in flats filled with a mixture of soil, sand, peat moss, and vermiculite. Plant seeds about 1/2 inch deep, 1 inch apart, water the planting medium thoroughly, and place the flat in a warm place, about 70 to 80 degrees. After 1 week, when the seeds have germinated, place the flat in a sunny window, southern exposure preferred. If you have Gro-Lux or fluorescent lights, place plants under them for about 12 to 14 hours a day.

One week before outdoor planting time, begin to harden off your plants, that is, prepare them for the rigors of outdoor weather. Place them outside in a sunny spot for a few days, and bring them in at night. Then, let them remain outside on warm nights as well. If a cold snap is forecast, bring them inside for protection. By the end of the week, you can leave them out overnight. On an overcast day, set them in the garden.

Be sure to fashion collars out of tin foil or cardboard to wrap around the stem of each plant as you set it in the ground. This precaution will save you from the disaster of a cutworm invasion.

Fertilize the ground sparingly with compost, rotted manure, and a handful of 5-10-5 fertilizer or organic mixture. Do not overfertilize, as too much nitrogen in the soil will cause the plants to go to leaf. Set plants in the soil with the lower leaves at plant level. Notice that this is deeper than the soil level of the indoor planting medium.

When the plants have grown about 1 foot high, drive a 5-foot stake into the ground about 4 inches from the main stem of the plant. As the tomato plants grow, tie them firmly to the stake.

Be sure to keep your bed free from weeds and provide plenty of moisture during drought, at least 1 1/2 inches of water per week.

PESTS: Tomato hornworms are green with diagonal lines on their sides and a prominent spike or horn on the rear. Hand-pick the worms and immerse in kerosene or bleach. If you choose to spray, a 50 percent Sevin WP (2 tablespoons to 1 gallon of water) should be applied as soon as these creatures appear. A 5 percent rotenone WP (5 tablespoons to 1 gallon of water) will keep flea beetles under control. These are pinhead size, black, brown, or striped, jumping beetles about 1/16 inch long.

VARIETIES: Roma, San Marzano.

COOKING TIP 1

Use these in any Italian tomato sauce recipe instead of canned tomatoes. And you *will* notice the difference.

PEAR TOMATOES

These are the pear shaped sweet as sugar tomatoes that have replaced the cherry tomatoes as the number one tomato for salads and hors doeuvres. I still grow the cherries, because they are quite early and satisfy that tomato yearning I get every year in early summer. But for mid and late season salads, the pear shaped tomatoes are superb.

HARDINESS: Annual, tender.

WHEN TO PLANT: Start seeds indoors 6 to 8 weeks before all danger of frost is past. Set outside mid-May to early June.

SPACING: Indoors: Sow 1 inch apart; outdoors: Plant seedlings about 1 foot apart.

DEPTH: Indoors: 1/2 inch; outdoors: Plant just below first pair of leaves on plant, regardless of soil line.

HARVEST TIME: 70 days.

HOW TO GROW PEAR TOMATOES: Culture is the same as for Cherry Tomatoes. See above.

GARDENER'S TIP 1

Pear Tomatoes also adapt nicely to tub planting and are quite decorative on porches and patios.

PESTS: Pests are the same as with Cherry Tomatoes. See above.

VARIETIES: Red Pear and Yellow Pear. The yellow version has a milder flavor.

HERBS

H E R B S

Y<small>OU ARE UNDOUBTEDLY FAMILIAR</small> with the difference in aroma between fresh home-dried herbs and spices and those bought in the grocery store. The difference they mae-make in the final taste of foods you prepare is equally dramatic. Yet growing herbs and spices is, for the most part, a simple matter. Most are disease and pest free and are vigorous growers.

Once you've started your collection, you'll want to add to it. Keep that in mind when planting, and allow space for the expansion of your herb garden.

There are just a few simple things that you should be aware of when it comes to growing herbs. First, moisture requirements. Since most herbs are native to the Mediterranean areas, they are very resistant to drought. This does not mean that in severe droughts you can ignore them, but they will almost always survive neglect and dry spells. In fact, if you overwater them, they are susceptible to root rot, as are any plants which prefer dry climates. Be sure you select an area of your garden which has good drainage, as water-logged soil will also encourage root rot. And, once a plant has root rot, you must dig it up and dispose of it.

Second is light requirement. Most herbs prefer full sun—6 to 8 hours a day of direct light—but many will grow and thrive in partial sunlight. Some will be happier than others in a somewhat shady spot; among these are the mints, chervil, sweet woodruff, tarragon, and sweet violets. Herbs do not, however, thrive in deep shade.

Many herbs like a relatively poor soil and will have stronger scents and flavors if not over-fertilized and coddled. This is truer of the small-leafed perennials, like tarragon and thyme, than of the more tender-leafed annuals, such as sweet basil.

Beyond root rot caused by overwatering, the only pests which occasionally attack herbs are white flies and aphids. And these primarily when you grow herbs indoors or in a greenhouse. To remove, either spray the infected plants with a strong stream of water to wash pests away or spray a mixture of 1 tablespoon detergent to one gallon of water. If you use soapy water, wash the leaves a day or so later to prevent the soap from damaging the leaves.

Whatever you do, do not spray herbs with chemicals, notably diazanon, marathon, pyrethrum and synthetic pyrethrum derivatives, no matter what you are told at garden centers, nurseries and even from personal friends. Remember that in most cases, you harvest the leaves of herbs for culinary use. Spraying with chemicals and then using leaves for cooking or steeping, can be hazardous to your health.

ANISE SEED

(Pimpinella animus)

Perennial anise has a flavored seed that is easily grown. It goes back to Virgil's time, when it was used in a spice cake eaten at the end of a meal in order to prevent indigestion. It was also served at the end of a marriage feast and is probably the origin of today's spicy wedding cake.

HARDINESS: Perennial, hardy.

WHEN TO PLANT: After all danger of frost, from mid-May to early June.

SPACING: Sow thinly and thin to 6 inches apart when seedlings are 2 inches high.

DEPTH: 1/4 inch.

HARVEST TIME: Mid to late summer, when flower heads dry.

HOW TO GROW ANISE SEED: Sow seeds thinly, about 1/4 inch deep, in full sun after all danger of frost. Thin to 6 inches apart and keep weeded and watered during the summer. Anise does best in soil that is not too rich, so don't add fertilizer to your bed. In mid to later summer, white or rose-pink flowers will appear. When the flower heads dry, pick them and rub out the seeds. Store them in airtight containers in a cool, dry place.

GARDENER'S TIP 1

Anise seed can be saved through the winter and planted the following spring.

PESTS: There are none.

VARIETY: Simply anise.

COOKING TIP 1

Anise seeds are traditionally used to add a licorice flavor to breads, cakes, cookies, and desserts. However, for a change of pace, when you prepare a compote of fresh or stewed fruits, simply put a few anise seeds into the sugar syrup when you cook it. It imparts a delicate taste to the fruit.

BASIL

(Ocimum basilica)

Basil has been called the "herb of kings," for it has been used in food cooked for royal personages since classical times. Undoubtedly you are familiar with it and probably have some on your spice shelf. Fresh basil is far superior to the dried variety for potent oils are lost in drying. Cultivation is simple. As you are undoubtedly aware, basil is basic to Italian cuisine, and Thai basil basic to Thai cuisine.

HARDINESS: Annual, tender.

WHEN TO PLANT: After all danger of frost, from mid-May to early June.

SPACING: In rows 2 feet apart, sow seeds about 1/2 inch apart, ultimately thinning to 8 inches apart.

DEPTH: 1/4 inch.

HARVEST TIME: Early in the season to thin your bed and then until frost.

HOW TO GROW BASIL: Plant basil when you plant your tomatoes, in mid-May to early June. And, in fact, if you plant some right next to your tomatoes, basil serves as a trap plant for pests which might infest them. Basil grows in full sun or semi-shade and needs only moderately fertile soil. Mix a little rotted manure, compost, or 5-10-5 fertilizer or organic mixture into your bed. Plant the seeds about 1/2 inch apart, 1/4 inch deep, in rows about 2 feet apart. After the seedlings emerge, thin to 8 inches apart. Use the seedlings in cooking. Then, pick leaves as you need them throughout the season.

GARDENER'S TIP 1

After the second set of leaves appear on your plant, pinch back the tips to increase bushiness.

GARDENER'S TIP 2

When the blossoms on your plants have just begun to open, take cuttings during the early morning for drying and winter storage. Rinse the leaves under cool water to remove the dirt and any insects that might be present and discard the damaged leaves. Then tie them with string and hang them upside down in the kitchen or any cool, dry place. Or spread them out on a screen or on cheesecloth in a dark, well-ventilated place away from direct sunlight to dry. Once dried, remove the leaves from the stems and store in airtight bottles in a cool, dark place for winter use.

GARDENER'S TIP 3

Be sure to let some of your crop go to seed. Collect the seed, store in a cool, dry place, and plant the following spring.

PESTS: Basil will ward off pests which attack other vegetables.

VARIETIES: Because of the popularity of basil, hybridizers and seed companies have been working overtime creating dozens of new basil varieties. Here are some of them:

Genovese Basil: 2 to 3 feet tall, with large dark green leaves about 2 inches long.

Genovese Compact Basil: 16-18 inches tall, more compact growing than standard basil.

Italian Large Leaf Basil: Slightly sweet, and very suitable for pesto, growing 2 to 3 feet tall, with large leaves.

Mammoth Basil: With gigantic, thick, glossy green leaves, similar to lettuce, but less crinkled. Sweet and spicy clove flavor. 16-20 inches tall.

Spicy Bush Basil: An 8 to 14-inch dwarf plant with very fine leaves. Also known as Greek basil.

Basil Finn Verde: 18-22 inches tall, very tiny leaves. Sweet and pungently spicy.

Cinnamon Basil: Very sweet cinnamon scent, can be used in herbal teas and potpourri. Violet stems. 26-30 inches tall.

Lemon-Scented Basil: Sweet, strong lemon aroma. Good for vinegar and fish. 18-22 inches tall.

Lime Basil: Distinct, zesty, lime aroma. Adds citrus flair to fish and salads. 20-26 inches tall.

Sweet Thai Basil: Strong, spicy, anise-clove scent for cooking. Used extensively in both Thai and Vietnamese cuisine. Small, green leaves, purple stems and blossoms. 12-18 inches tall.

Holy Basil: Revered by Hindus, and called Capri in Thailand. Musky scent with a hint of mint. 20-24 inches tall.

Osmium Purple Basil: Very dark, purple leaves and stems. Glossy, slightly ruffled, purple leaves on a sturdy plant. 18-24 inches tall.

Red Ruben Basil: Very large leafed purple basil. 18-24 inches.

Purple Ruffles Basil: Large ruffled purple leaves. One of the most popular basils. Grows 16-20 inches tall.

COOKING TIP 1

Sweet basil leaves are used in vinegar, stews, fish, salads, tomato dishes, spaghetti, vegetable juices, and butter sauces. Tea made from the leaves is calming to the nerves.

COOKING TIP 2

Perhaps the most delicious way to enjoy basil is in Italian pesto. In Genoa, where this delicious sauce originated, they insist that it can be made only with a marble mortar. However, a delicious version can also be made either in a blender or food processor as well. You'll need 2 whole cups of basil leaves to make this wonderful concoction. You can serve it on fettucine, with potato gnocchi, or mixed into a hot or cold minestrone.

BORAGE

(Brag officials)

Borage is a largely undiscovered herb that adds a cooling touch to summer drinks and desserts. It should be grown more widely as it is an almost indestructible addition to any herb garden and provides a hit of spectacular blue when in bloom.

HARDINESS: Annual tender.

WHEN TO PLANT: In spring after all danger of frost.

SPACING: 20 inches apart.

DEPTH: 1/4 inch.

HARVEST TIME: Throughout season as plant grows.

HOW TO GROW BORAGE: Plant in full sun or partial shade. Will thrive in poor soil with moderate, but consistent watering.

GARDENER'S TIP 1

Borage can be invasive if allowed to self sow seeds in fall. To contain it, collect all seed pods and plant where you want it to grow.

PESTS: There are none.

VARIETIES: Simply Borage.

COOKING TIP 1

Beyond the refreshing qualities of the foliage, from late spring to late fall, bear small star-shaped flowers which begin pink and mature to a fabulous saturated blue which can be used to add elegant touches as garnish for summer drinks, salads and even sorbets. The whole flower can be eaten, but it is more delicate if you carefully remove the brightly colored flower from its hairy green sepal, attempting to keep the star-shaped flower intact.

Cooking Tip 2

Scatter flowers over a platter of sliced tomatoes. They add a slightly bitter, cucumber flavor to the tomatoes and a sea-blue accent to the gorgeous red of an impeccably ripe tomato.

Cooking Tip 3

A version of the classic English watercress sandwiches can be made with Borage. Mix Borage leaves with cream cheese and mayonnaise and spread on thin slices of bread. A perfect accompaniment for a pitcher of summer ice tea.

Caper Bush

(Capers spinosa)

Caper bushes are native to the warm, dry, sunny Mediterranean areas where they spring from the cracks in old sun-warmed walls. And so, they are appropriate choices for the southwestern areas of the United States and for southern California. The plants are not easy to find, but if you can locate one, they make an interesting warm-climate shrub.

HARDINESS: Perennial to Zone 8.

WHEN TO PLANT: Spring, after all danger of cold weather, or fall.

SPACING: 3-5 feet.

DEPTH: At soil level in pot.

HARVEST TIME: In summer when fruit appears on bush.

HOW TO GROW CAPERS: If the climate is right for them, that is dry sunny and warm, capers are easily grown. Plant them and water them occasionally and collect the small flower buds as they appear. Small white flowers from 2-3 inches across adorn the plant. The flower buds are pickled and eaten.

Gardener's Tip 1

Capers are not generally grown in the United States. However, if you can find a source for them, they are well worth the effort, just to have a large supply of the pickled flower buds.

PESTS: There are none.

VARIETIES: Simply caper bush.

Cooking Tip 1

My good friend and colleague Harry Haralambou, grew up in Cyprus. He recalls capers growing wild along the roadsides in the mountain village where he comes from. He used to pick them, and his sisters would pickle them. To pickle, use a combination of vinegar, pickling spices and water, and let buds steep for several weeks.

Caraway Seed

(Carum carvi)

Caraway seed is particularly prized for flavoring breads and rolls. Native to Northern Europe, it is also used in adding flavor to liqueurs. It is easily grown in the United States.

HARDINESS: Biennial, hardy.

WHEN TO PLANT: After all danger of frost, from mid-May to early June.

SPACING: Sow thinly and thin to 6 inches apart when seedlings are 1 inch high.

DEPTH: 1/4 inch.

HARVEST TIME: Since caraway is biennial, plant one year and harvest the seeds the following year.

HOW TO GROW CARAWAY SEED: Sow seeds in full sun, about 1/4 inch deep. When plants are about 1 inch high, thin them to 6 inches apart. Nurture plants during the season, watering them regularly, and keep your patch weed-free. The following spring a sturdy stand of caraway will grow. By July or August, the plants will grow to a height of about 2 feet. White flowers in umbrels will adorn them. Eventually these will go to seed and your caraway seed crop will be ready to harvest. Collect the seed, place in airtight containers, and store in a cool, dark, dry place.

Gardener's Tip 1

Be advised that caraway has a tendency to take over a garden, so you must be ruthless in restricting your crop to its allocated patch. Simply dig out or plow under any unwanted plants.

Gardener's Tip 2

Once you've collected your harvest, be sure to save enough seed for the following 2 years. Plant each year, for the following year's crop.

PESTS: There are none.

VARIETY: Simply caraway.

Cooking Tip 1

In Belgium, caraway seed is added to the cooking water when Brussels sprouts are prepared. The taste complements the vegetables perfectly. Since caraway is a member of the carrot family, the slender taproot is very tasty and edible. You can also chop the leaves and add these to salads or soups. An exceptional hors doeuvre spread can be made by combining 1/3 cup crumbled blue cheese, 1/3 cup mayonnaise, 3 ounces cream cheese, 2 teaspoons caraway seed, and 1/4 teaspoon freshly ground pepper.

CATNIP

(Nepeta cataria)

Well, after all, we can't forget old Puss, now can we? No need to tell you that catnip is a wonderful treat for your feline friends. Its easily grown and virtually indestructible. My cats, Betty Boop, Naughty Lola and Josephine all enjoy catnip. And some dogs, like my cockapoo, Mr. Chips, enjoy it as well.

HARDINESS: Perennial, hardy.

WHEN TO PLANT: From early spring through midsummer.

SPACING: Sow thinly in rows about 1 foot apart.

DEPTH: 1/4 inch.

HARVEST TIME: All through the season.

HOW TO GROW CATNIP: From early spring to midsummer, purchase plants from your local garden center or through a mail order nursery. If you opt for plants, just set them in the ground, water them, and keep them weed-free. You can also grow catnip from seed. Plant thinly in rows about 1 foot apart, 1/4 inch deep. Catnip will thrive in full sun or partial shade and is not the slightest fussy about soil. You can pick the leaves for your cat through the season and then dry them in fall for winter use. To dry, cut the stems before the plant flowers, tie them with a string, and hang them upside down in a cool, dry, shady place. In several weeks the leaves will dry out and you can store them as a treat for Puss during the winter.

GARDENER'S TIP 1
Catnip adapts very well to pot culture, so at the end of the season, pot some and grow it in a sunny window for winter use.

PESTS: There are none.

VARIETY: Catnip.

COOKING TIP 1
After you've satisfied Puss, you can make herbal tea for human consumption. It is best mixed with dried peppermint and lemon balm. Some say it encourages latent tendencies of curiosity.

CHERVIL

(Anthriscus cerefolium)

Chervil is relatively unknown in the United States. However, it is used extensively as salad material and in the preparation of elegant sauces on the Continent. It's easily grown if you observe the instructions for germinating difficult seeds. It tastes like a mild tarragon.

HARDINESS: Annual, very hardy.

WHEN TO PLANT: In early spring when ground is workable.

SPACING: In rows 1 foot apart, plants 8 inches apart.

DEPTH: 1/8 inch.

HARVEST TIME: 50 to 75 days.

HOW TO GROW CHERVIL: Chervil, like parsley, is hardy to cold but sensitive to heat. Therefore, plant early, the same time you plant peas, lettuce, and onions. Full sun, fertile soil, and reasonable moisture are necessary for a fine crop. The trick to growing chervil is the same as that for growing parsley. Germination is slow, and unless you keep your bed well watered, your crop will fail. To overcome this, soak the seeds in water overnight about 2 weeks before planting. After that place the seeds on a damp paper towel, fold the towel up with the contained seeds, and place in the refrigerator until they germinate (about 1 to 2 weeks).

Then sow the seeds thinly in the garden, about 1/8 inch deep, two per inch. After they have grown to a height of about 2 inches, thin them to about 6 inches apart. Pick the leaves as you need them, for others will grow in their place.

GARDENER'S TIP 1

Chervil can be moved indoors during the winter. Simply pot a plant and place it in a sunny window and enjoy fresh chervil throughout the colder months.

GARDENER'S TIP 2

You can also dry chervil. Pick a supply early in the morning, tie the leaves together with a string, and hang the bundle upside down in a dry, airy place. The leaves should dry out in about 2 weeks. Then crumble the leaves, remove the brittle stems, and store in an airtight container in a cool, dry, dark place.

PESTS: There are none.

VARIETY: Simply chervil.

COOKING TIP 1

Many classic French and Belgian fish sauces call for chervil. It is also delicious in soup and salad. For a special treat, check out any recipe for watercress soup and substitute chervil for the cress, and you'll understand why Belgian cuisine is considered by many to be the finest on earth.

COOKING TIP 2

In the Province district of France a very popular salad called mesclun is made by mixing the leaves of chervil, arugula, leaf lettuce, and fine-curled endive. In fact, to facilitate picking, the seeds of the four leafy vegetables are mixed together and sowed as one. They are picked at a very, very young stage and prepared with various salad dressings.

Chives

(Allium schoenoprasum)

Chives are very easy to grow. For added pleasure, in the spring, lovely purple flowers adorn the plants. One of the first of all herbs to emerge in the spring, chive adds a fresh taste to so many foods. No gourmet should be without this useful herb.

HARDINESS: Perennial, very hardy.

WHEN TO PLANT: In early spring, when ground is workable.

SPACING: In rows 1 foot apart, sow seeds thinly about 1/4 inch apart. Thin to 1 foot.

DEPTH: About 1/4 inch.

HARVEST TIME: Throughout the season.

HOW TO GROW CHIVE: Chive is fussy about soil. Any reasonably fertile soil is suitable. Plant in full sun or semi-shade. Sow the seeds as early in the spring as ground is workable. Plant thinly, about 1/4 inch apart, 1/4 inch deep. Cover the seeds with fine soil, tamp down, and water gently. In about 2 weeks your seedlings will emerge from the ground. When the plants are about 3 inches high, thin to 1 foot apart. A short row of about 5 feet should provide you with more than enough of this herb. After plants have matured, you can transplant some to your kitchen door area so that they are convenient for picking, as you will find many uses for this member of the onion family. Every few years, dig the plants, divide, and replant.

GARDENER'S TIP 1

If you permit the purple flowers to go to seed, the plant will reseed itself prodigiously. To keep your garden tidy, pick off the flowers before they fade. They are edible and look attractive in a salad bowl.

GARDENER'S TIP 2

In the fall, pick enough chive for winter use. Cut the chive with scissors and freeze for relatively fresh herbs during the winter.

GARDENER'S TIP 3

Chives grow vigorously in pots, so in the fall, dig a small plant, pot it, and place in a sunny windowsill during the winter.

PESTS: There are none.

VARIETIES: Simply Chive.

COOKING TIP 1

Chive combines marvelously with many foods, but few cooks blend them into a sauce. A simple buerre blanc, fortified with chopped chive, is elegant and memorable.

CILANTRO

(CORIANDER OR CHINESE PARSLEY)

(Coriandrum sativum)

The seeds of this plant are known as coriander, while the leaves are known as Cilantro or Chinese Parsley. The leaves are used extensively in Mediterranean and Chinese dishes and are indispensible to good Mexican cooking. Cilantro is easily grown from seed and grows on a single stem, 2-3 feet high.

HARDINESS: Annual, tender.

WHEN TO PLANT: In spring, after all danger of frost.

SPACING: About 2-3 inches apart.

DEPTH: Sow seeds about 1/4 inch deep.

HARVEST TIME: When plants are 6 inches tall, you can begin to cut foliage. Continue throughout summer and fall.

HOW TO GROW CILANTRO: Plant in full sun or partial shade in moderately rich soil with good drainage. Seeds germinate quickly. Tall stems may need staking.

GARDENER'S TIP 1

Plant every 2-3 weeks, as cilantro bolts rapidly when the weather grows warm. At the end of the season allow a few plants to cast seed and you will have hardy volunteers very early the following spring.

PESTS: There are none.

VARIETIES: Simply Cilantro or Coriander.

COOKING TIP 1

The leaves have a distinctive flavor which for some is an acquired taste. Once acquired however, it can be addictive. It is essential to the classic Mexican fresh table sauce, or salsa—the one that always comes to the table with huaraches and sopas and tostadas or just with crisply fried tortillas as an appetizer. To make basic salsa cruda, mince or mash 3 to 4 cloves garlic with a sprinkling of coarse salt (in a Mexican kitchen this is done in a molcajete or rough-bottomed mortar). Add 3 fully ripe tomatoes, peeled, seeded, and chopped. Add finely chopped strong white onion, chopped cilantro, and minced fresh jalapeño peppers to taste. Squeeze some fresh lemon or lime juice over and sprinkle with freshly ground black pepper. The salsa becomes more liquid as the ingredients release their essences.

COOKING TIP 2

Combine the flavor of fresh cilantro leaves with minced lemon grass, ginger root, a pinch of crushed red chili pepper, garlic, and chicken broth to make the base for many Thai-influenced soups and noodle dishes. If you can get hold of a Kaffir lime leaf to toss in, so much the better.

DILL

(Anethum graveolens)

Dill is one of the most versatile herbs grown. It is used widely in the cuisine of Scandinavia, Poland, Hungary, and Czechoslovakia. No gourmet garden should be without this delightful treasure. If you do any pickling at all, you know that dill is basic.

HARDINESS: Annual, hardy.

WHEN TO PLANT: In early spring, when ground is workable.

SPACING: Sow seed thinly and thin to 3 or 4 inches apart as season progresses.

DEPTH: 1/2 inch.

HARVEST TIME: Throughout the season for fresh dill and at the end of the season for seeds and dried dill weed.

HOW TO GROW DILL: Sow seeds thinly, 1/2 inch deep and thin to about 3 or 4 inches apart during the season. Dill is not fussy about soil and is pest-free, but full sun is required. Keep in mind that this herb, with its feathery leaves, grows to a height of about 2 feet, so plan accordingly in your garden. To protect plants from wind damage you can plant in a circle. Dill dislikes being transplanted.

Harvest the leaves as you need them during the season and in the fall be sure to gather seeds for baking and flavoring various dishes. Save some for planting the following spring, but it often self-seeds.

GARDENER'S TIP 1

To dry dill weed, pick a supply early in the morning, tie the leaves with a string, and hang upside down in a dry, shady, airy place. The leaves should dry out in about 2 weeks. Crumble the leaves, removing the brittle stems, and store them in an airtight container in a cool, dry, dark place.

PESTS: There are none.

VARIETY: Dill.

Here's an authentic recipe for making kosher dill pickles: Pack pickling cucumbers as tightly as possible in a quart jar. Add 3 to 4 sprigs dill, 1 large pinch pickling spices, 1 clove garlic, and 1 bay leaf. Fill jars with strong salt water solution (1/3 cup kosher salt to 1 quart water heated until salt dissolves). Cover and let sit at room temperature until pickled to taste. Try after 4 days. If you like stronger pickles let sit a few more days. When desired strength is attained, store in refrigerator. You can also process these pickles.

LEMON GRASS

(Cymbopogon citratus)

Lemon Grass is native to tropical Southeast Asia and grows in clumps of up to 6 feet, if conditions are ideal. However, in southern parts of the United States it generally grows from 2-3 feet high. Grass-like leaves are 3 feet long, dark green, about 1/2 inch wide.

HARDINESS: Perennial, tender to Zone 8.

WHEN TO PLANT: Plant in spring after all danger of frost.

SPACING: 5 feet.

DEPTH: At level of plant in pot.

HARVEST TIME: All year long.

HOW TO GROW LEMON GRASS: It is best to purchase plants from a nursery or a mail order source. although native to tropical regions, it can easily be grown as a potted plant in cooler climates and can be wintered indoors. From Zone 8 south, you can leave it in the garden all winter. Prefers partial shade and rich well-drained soil.

If you want to propagate plants from an established clump, do so in the spring. Before digging clumps, cut the leaves to a few inches above the root. Then plant clumps in soil as above. Be sure that a few inches of the leaf remain above the soil. Water sparingly but mist leaves often. Do not fertilize. Trim leaves to encourage growth.

PESTS: There are none.

VARIETIES: Simply lemon grass.

COOKING TIP 1

Lemon grass is used in many Oriental dishes and is a staple in Thai cuisine. Cut leaves can be dried or frozen, and retain their piquant lemony flavor. Toss a few leaves into the pot when you are making homemade chicken stock; like bay leaves, they need time to infuse their flavor into the stock.

COOKING TIP 2

For quick lemon grass flavor, very finely mince the bulb-like base of a fresh stalk or stem and add it directly to the dish you are cooking.

COOKING TIP 3

Infuse bulbs of lemon grass in good-quality white wine vinegar for an interesting, tangy flavored vinegar. Some cooks add garlic and hot red chiles to this combination. The resulting vinegar makes a useful addition for seafood dishes, vinaigrettes, and creamy dressings for artichokes or potato salad.

LEMON VERBENA

(Aloysia triphylla)

The heavenly scent of Lemon Verbena is more than just lemon. It is the apotheosis of lemon. Lemon taken and elevated to near nirvana. Used in cooking and as an unforgettable scent, it is irresistible and very elegant. The Guerlain perfume company created a lemon verbena cologne for Napoleon back in the early part of the 19th century. It is called Imperiale and costs about $150 a bottle. You can approximate the scent by simply picking leaves of your homegrown plant and rubbing them on your skin. However be advised that admirers both private and public are driven into frenzies of desire when they catch the scent of a gentle whiff of lemon verbena on your body. Plan accordingly.

HARDINESS: Perennial only to Zone 8. Farther north treat as annual.

WHEN TO PLANT: In spring after all danger of frost.

SPACING: About 3 feet apart.

DEPTH: Plant at level of growth in container.

HARVEST TIME: Early in the season when plant begins to grow pick sparingly, then through summer and fall pick as much as you need.

HOW TO GROW LEMON VERBENA: It is best to buy pots of this plant at nurseries or through mail order sources in early spring. You will not have luck growing this from seed. Prefers full sun, good well drained soil, but does resist drought. It adapts well to container planting and if you live in a cool climate, you can bring the plant indoors over the winter. It will lose its leaves, and you should water it sparingly, and then in the spring return it to its outdoor location.

Gardener's Tip 1

Keep the plant bushy and dense by carefully and regularly pinching and pruning. It likes to sprawl if left to its own devices.

PESTS: There are none.

VARIETIES: Simply Lemon Verbena.

Cooking Tip 1

My friend John Greene, who is an expert cook and charming host, suggests this use for Lemon Verbena. When you make tea for a cool iced drink, while tea is still hot, steep lemon verbena leaves in the water. When tea cools and is iced, the verbena taste is evident.

Cooking Tip 2

Certainly a near preposterously elegant use of lemon verbena, is to sprinkle some chopped and whole leaves on a refreshing summery lemon sorbet. Try it, this one will either knock the socks off your guests or you will never live it down. Either way, it's wonderful.

LOVAGE

(Levisticum officinale)

Lovage self sows vigorously once established, so unless you collect the seeds from plants at the end of the season, and plant them where you want them, you will have them all over the place.

HARDINESS: Perennial, hardy to Zone 4.

WHEN TO PLANT: Plant fresh seeds every fall. Germination is spotty, so plant thickly.

SPACING: Thin seedlings to about 3 feet apart.

DEPTH: About 1/4 inch.

HARVEST TIME: Foliage can be used all during the season, stems at the end of the season and seeds when they have formed on the plant in the fall.

PESTS: There are none.

VARIETIES: Simply lovage.

COOKING TIP 1

Lovage is an amalgam of flavors, primarily celery and parsley. For this reason anytime a dish calls for aromatics, add some lovage to the pot. It is good in salads, soups, stews, vegetables, meats, poultry and sauces. You can also blanch the stems and eat as a vegetable. Seeds can be used sprinkled on meat, bread, cookies or in vegetables, such as carrots or spinach. Some say that chopped lovage leaves mixed with cream cheese make the most delightful sandwich filling they know.

MARJORAM

(Oreganum majorana)

The confusion between sweet marjoram and oregano continues unabated. For centuries the two have been used interchangeably, with a taste difference so subtle that only those with the most discerning palate will be able to sense it. Marjoram is a shade sweeter in flavor and slightly more delicate. It can also have a pungent, camphor-like overtone more shrill than the scent and flavor of Oregano. Both Oregano and Marjoram are perennial though Marjoram is tender at temperatures below 20° F. Oregano is slightly difficult to raise from seed, so if potted plants are not available, Sweet Marjoram is a good substitute. It grows to about two feet high, resembling an upright shrub. Stems are reddish and fuzzy foliage is from 3/4 to 1-1/2 inches long. A low growing form, creeping golden marjoram, is useful in the landscape because of its lovely color.

HARDINESS: Annual, tender.

WHEN TO PLANT: Spring.

SPACING: Thin to from 6-8 inches apart.

DEPTH: About 1/4 inch.

HARVEST TIME: Early in the season to thin your bed and then until frost.

HOW TO GROW SWEET MARJORAM: Sow seeds in full sun after all danger of frost. Plant in rich, light well-drained soil. To encourage bushiness, cut back before white flower clusters appear. Pick leaves as needed, though flavor seems to be most intense before the white flower clusters appear.

GARDENER'S TIP 1

Marjoram seed can be saved through the winter for subsequent spring planting.

PESTS: There are none.

VARIETY: Simply marjoram.

COOKING TIP 1

Marjoram is one of the herbs used in the well known French combination called fines herbs, often called for in omelets. You can also use it as you would oregano. Marjoram is an excellent compliment to tomato based dishes, is used to add zest to salads, and combines well with the mild cabbage taste of Brussels Sprouts.

COOKING TIP 2

Marjoram is another herb which can be dug in the fall before frost, potted up and grown on a sunny windowsill all winter long.

MINTS

(Mentha)

Useful and pleasant, easy-going, wonderful for its ambient perfume, mint surely has a place in your herb garden. And it comes in lots of flavors besides the familiar spearmint and peppermint.

HARDINESS: Perennial, hardy.

WHEN TO PLANT: From early spring to fall.

SPACING: 2 feet apart.

DEPTH: At soil level of purchased stock.

HARVEST TIME: Throughout the growing season.

HOW TO GROW MINT: Just about infallible, given a minimum of attention. Just plant in sun or shade from spring to fall and water until established. The mints are not fussy about soil.

Gardener's Tip 1

All mints should be picked when young. As they grow older, they lose a substantial amount of their delightful taste.

Gardener's Tip 2

Mints will run rampant if given a chance. I have found the best way to contain them is to plant them in large plastic tubs and sink the tubs into the soil. If not kept in hand, they will take over your entire garden within a few years.

Gardener's Tip 3

Purchase plants of these mints from mail order houses or nurseries. Or ask friends for a snip. Growing from seed can be difficult.

PESTS: There are no pests, however rust spots may develop on foliage during hot weather. This does not affect the underground runners or stems, nor does it affect the new emerging shoots. It also does not affect the taste of the mint. If it bothers you, just cut the infected shoots to the ground and let new growth replace it.

VARIETIES:

Apple mint: An apple-like scent and flavor. Grows into a tall, woolly plant.

Lemon mint: As its name implies, a lemony taste.

Orange mint: This has a pleasant orange-like flavor.

Peppermint: The common, tangy mint so well known.

Pineapple mint: One of my favorites, with a mild pineapple scent and a beautiful growth habit.

Spearmint: Somewhat strong. Useful if you make your own toothpaste or chewing gum.

Cooking Tip 1

We all know that mint is a traditional garnish for iced tea, lemonade, and other summer beverages. However, it serves well in hot winter beverages as well. Beyond the mint teas, try adding some dried mint leaves to hot chocolate. It's a very soothing cold-weather delight. And in summer, add fresh mint to cold chocolate. Its delicious in yogurt dressings and in tabouli, the tangy Middle Eastern salad made with bulgur wheat.

OREGANO

(Origanum)

Oregano is probably best known as the herb which Italians use in spaghetti sauce, pizza, and other dishes. However, you might be surprised to learn that there are many other uses for this versatile herb. For better flavored oregano, grow your own. There is no comparison between the fresh version and the store-bought product. There are many which are grown throughout the world, some of which are not botanically of the same family. Crete dittany, *O. dictamnus,* has thick silvery fuzzy, almost round leaves. Flowers are purple. Fresh or dry leaves can be used for tea or seasoning. *Coleus amboinicus,* also called Cuban oregano, Spanish Thyme or Virgin Island oregano has thick fleshy stems that are used fresh in the same way that common oregano is used. Mexican oregano, *Lippia graveolens* or *L. palmeri,* is similar to true oregano, so much so that commercial herb growers do not distinguish between the two.

HARDINESS: Perennial.

WHEN TO PLANT: From late spring to early fall.

SPACING: About 2 feet apart.

DEPTH: At soil level of plant in pot.

HARVEST TIME: Start picking leaves around the middle of June and continue throughout the summer.

HOW TO GROW OREGANO: Your best bet is to purchase plants from a nursery or mail order house. You can grow this herb from seed, but if you do, you will have to start by planting indoors long before the growing season. If you opt for plants, set them in the ground at soil level, about 2 feet apart, after all danger of frost is over, from mid-May to early June. Plant in full sun and well-drained soil. Aside from that, the needs of oregano are few.

GARDENER'S TIP 1

Oregano has a spreading tendency, so be sure to control your bed.

GARDENER'S TIP 2

Take advantage of the spreading habit and plant in a rock garden, on a slope, or along garden paths.

GARDENER'S TIP 3

Dry some oregano for winter use. Pick early in the day, tie with a string, and hang upside down in a cool, dry, shady place until thoroughly dry. Then remove leaves and discard woody stems, place in airtight containers, and store in a cool, shady, dry place.

PESTS: There are no serious pests.

COOKING TIP 1

Of course, use oregano in Italian cuisine. However, the next time you prepare pot roast, rub the entire piece of meat with fresh or dried oregano. The flavor imparted is delicious.

PARSLEY

French Curled and Italian (Petroselinum crispum)

Two kinds of parsley are used in the preparation of gourmet foods. French curled parsley is used primarily for garnish, although it can be used in cooking or salad. The Italian or flat-leafed parsley is said to be far more intense in flavor and is consequently used more commonly in gourmet cooking. Both are easily grown if you know the simple trick of speeding up seed germination.

HARDINESS: Grow as annual, but will grow as biennial, that is it will grow the first year, winter over on its own and then grow the second year, before dying from winterkill.

WHEN TO PLANT: In early spring when ground is workable.

SPACING: In rows 1 foot apart, sow seeds thinly.

DEPTH: 1/8 inch.

HARVEST TIME: From 50 to 75 days.

HOW TO GROW PARSLEY: Parsley is hardy to cold but sensitive to heat. It thrives on conditions similar to those for growing kale, lettuce, and spinach. And, if given a little protection, you can often carry it over the winter, affording fresh parsley leaves very early in the spring.

Parsley thrives in any good soil. Cut during the early stages of its growth, it is very delicate, so a finely powdered, friable soil is preferable.

It is best to buy parsley plants at your local garden center or nursery, but if you wish to grow them from seed, be aware that it is somewhat complicated. The most common problem with failure of a parsley crop involves the germination of the tiny seeds. They are extremely slow in germinating, sometimes taking more than a month. The secret to success is to put them in the freezer for a few days, then soak the seeds in water overnight about 1 week before planting time. After then, place the seeds on a damp paper towel, fold the towel up with the contained seeds, place in a plastic sandwich bag, and put in the refrigerator. After about a week, the tiny seeds will germinate and you can plant them directly in your garden.

Sow thinly, six seeds per inch, about 1/8 inch deep in full sun. When the plants are 2 to 3 inches high, thin them to 6 inches apart. Pick the leaves as you need them, for others will grow in their place.

Gardener's Tip 1
You can plant a crop of parsley in the fall, mulch it heavily to protect from the extreme cold of winter, and then in spring remove mulch.

Gardener's Tip 2
For a continuous supply of parsley during the winter, dig a plant, pot it, and place it on a sunny windowsill. Your parsley should thrive. If you have a cat, you might find that she will nibble at your plant, so provide some sort of protection.

PESTS: Depending on your locality, parsley worm can be a problem. Inquire locally for control information.

VARIETIES: Extra Curled Dwarf is the French variety; Plain or Single is the Italian.

COOKING TIP 1

In addition to using parsley as garnish and in cooking, many Continental cooks and Thai cooks lightly fry parsley in oil and serve it with fish or vegetables. Simply place a handful of stalks in hot oil for a few seconds, remove, drain, and serve immediately. This will add a very elegant touch to your entrees.

ROSEMARY

(Rosmarinum officinalis)

Another of the staple herbs for gourmet cooking, the aromatic rosemary is used in many classic dishes made with lamb and chicken.

HARDINESS: Perennial in the South and, with protection in the winter, sometimes perennial in the North. To be sure of a crop, grow as an annual in the North, from a plant rather than from seed.

WHEN TO PLANT: In spring after all danger of frost, from mid-May to early June.

SPACING: Sow sparsely and thin to 6 to 8 inches apart when 2 inches high.

DEPTH: 1/2 inch.

HARVEST TIME: Fresh during the season and for drying in the fall.

HOW TO GROW ROSEMARY: Plant in spring when all danger of frost is over, from mid-May to early June. Sow seeds thinly, 1/2 inch deep, and when plants are 2 inches high, thin to 6 to 8 inches apart. Rosemary is not fussy about soil, but reasonable sunshine is a requirement. The plant is handsome, resembling a small pine tree. Harvest throughout the season as needed or cut dry in the fall. Tie in bunches and hang upside down in a cool, shady, dry place to dry. After 2 weeks or so, when thoroughly dry, store in airtight containers in a cool, dry, dark place.

GARDENER'S TIP 1

Rosemary can be incorporated into a border or flower bed, for its decorative foliage and lovely blue flowers are very attractive. The prostrate variety is perfect for a rock garden on a slope, as where the plant is perennial it will eventually cascade downward in billowing shapes covered by sky-blue flowers in early summer. The plant is a tender perennial, and will survive to approximately 20° F.

GARDENER'S TIP 2

If you live in the North and wish to try to winter over this plant, locate it near a south wall or in a sheltered spot, or pot up and bring inside. Mulch heavily after the first killing frost and you will probably succeed.

GARDENER'S TIP 3

A perennial rosemary bed needs a fairly heavy annual pruning to keep it in good shape. The dried pruned branches make a fragrant fire when tossed on the barbecue grill prior to grilling fish or chicken.

PESTS: Spittlebugs can be a problem where rosemary is perennial.

VARIETY: Rosemary. There is also a prostrate variety available.

COOKING TIP 1

You can turn plain old breaded zucchini or eggplant into something special by adding about 1 teaspoon crushed rosemary leaves to 1 cup bread crumbs

Saffron Crocus

(Crocus sativus)

Saffron is often called the king of spices. It is frightfully expensive for it takes an entire field of flowers to produce a small amount of dried saffron. 40,000 flowers are needed to make a mere one pound. However, for home use, you can grow these crocus and then pick the golden stigmas from the lovely blue or pale purple flower while in bloom. Remember that the spring blooming crocus is not a source of saffron. *Crocus sativus* alone offers this expensive spice.

HARDINESS: Perennial, hardy.

WHEN TO PLANT: Either in September or in early spring. Usually corms, similar to bulbs, are not available in spring.

SPACING: 4 inches.

DEPTH: 6 inches.

TIME TO HARVEST: In fall when plants bloom.

HOW TO GROW SAFFRON: It's easy. Dig a hole about 6 inches deep, place the corm in the hole, cover and a few weeks later the foliage and then flowers will appear.

Gardener's Tip 1
Order corms by August, and plant them immediately in soil. They will send forth shoots and flowers within a few weeks.

PESTS: There are none.

VARIETIES: Simply Crocus sativus.

Cooking Tip 1
Yes, it is a traditional ingredient in French bouillabaisse, Spanish paella, Swedish and Cornish saffron breads. Here's another nice use for it. When you make a grilled cheese sandwich or an Italian mozzarella *en carozza* (a grilled bread and mozzarella sandwich), put a pinch of saffron in the butter or oil you use to fry the sandwich. Suddenly a simple grilled cheese sandwich becomes a great treat.

SAGE

(Salvia)

Sage is another of the staple herbs used in cooking, both "gourmet" and "plain." Again, as with all herbs, the home-grown fresh variety is far superior to the dried versions available in the markets. Sage dries well for winter use.

HARDINESS: Perennial, hardy.

WHEN TO PLANT: In early spring, as soon as ground is workable.

SPACING: Set plants about 2 feet apart.

DEPTH: Plant to soil line on stock.

HARVEST TIME: Throughout season when needed and in fall for drying.

HOW TO GROW SAGE: Purchase plants from a nursery or reliable mail order house. Sage is not fussy about soil, though it prefers well-drained loam. Plant your sage in full sun, giving it plenty of space. Cultivate during the season to keep weed-free, and water during extreme dry spells. You won't be able to harvest a substantial amount of this herb until the third year or so, but once mature, a generous supply will be available to you all during the season. Harvest fresh leaves throughout the season and pick a supply to dry for winter use.

GARDENER'S TIP 1

Sage tends to be invasive, so be sure to keep your plants in bounds. You can plant your sage in a plastic tub and sink it into the ground.

GARDENER'S TIP 2

You can divide your plants every few years should you need a larger supply. Dig the plant in the spring, divide it into two or three separate plants, and replant.

Gardener's Tip 3

To dry, pick early in the morning in the early fall, tie leaves together, and hang upside down in a cool, airy, shaded place until dry. Then store in airtight containers in a cool, dark, dry place.

Gardener's Tip 4

Plant pineapple sage, if you wish, for its fragrance and its lovely growth habit, but don't expect to cook with it. It has little or no flavor. Stick with the culinary sages for cooking.

PESTS: There are none.

VARIETIES: Dwarf Vatican Sage: This miniature traces its origins to the Vatican gardens. Emperor Sage is a large plant with deep purple leaves. Holts Mammoth has the most intense flavor. It is grown commercially. Red Tricolor has a white pointed leaf with red and purple coloration.

Cooking Tip 1

Sage is good with pork or beef and in jellies and teas.

SAVORY, SUMMER

(Satureja hortensis)

Summer savory is an excellent addition to the herb garden because it offers a somewhat unique peppery taste. It is native to the Mediterranean area. The Romans used it to flavor vinegar and Pliny planted it near his apiary to improve the bees' honey. It grows to about 18 inches with a loose habit. Gray-green leaves are about one inch long, aromatic and tinged with purple in late summer. White to pink blossoms sport on the stems at the end of the growing season. Can be used in the landscape.

HARDINESS: Annual, tender.

WHEN TO PLANT: After all danger of frost, from mid-May to early June in most parts of the country.

SPACING: Thin to 8 inches apart.

DEPTH: About 1/4 inch.

HARVEST TIME: Early in the season to thin your bed and then until frost.

HOW TO GROW SUMMER SAVORY: Plant summer savory in early spring after all danger of frost. Select a site with full sun and well-drained soil, rich in organic matter. When plants are two inches tall, thin to around 6 inches apart. Use cuttings in cooking.

GARDENER'S TIP 1

If planted among beans, summer savory will keep white flies away.

PESTS: There are none.

VARIETY: Simply summer savory.

COOKING TIP 1

The leaves of summer savory have a peppery taste and add interesting zest to fresh and dry beans, cabbage and sauerkraut. It can also be used for flavoring vinegar. Savory also adds zip to Chinese stir-fried dishes and enhances the taste of poultry and fish.

COOKING TIP 2

Surprisingly enough the peppery scent of savory is an interesting addition to homemade potpourris. In the fall the foliage turns a deep purple and the plant sports tiny lavender flowers. Hang and dry these and use them for indoor fall decoration.

COOKING TIP 3

Dried savory is a good soup seasoning for winter, and works nicely with pork chops and egg dishes, too. Start with sparing amounts until you decide if the flavor is for you and how much of it appeals to you in your winter "comfort dishes."

Savory, Winter
(Satureja montana)

Winter savory is very similar to summer savory and will grow as a perennial in all but the very coldest parts of the country. Thus, if you wish to save the trouble of planting the annual summer variety every year, purchase plants of winter savory. All information about summer savory is also true of winter savory.

HARDINESS: Perennial.

WHEN TO PLANT: Is best grown from plants purchased either from nurseries or mail order sources. Plant in spring after all danger of frost, from Mid-May to June in most parts of the country.

SPACING: 6-9 inches apart.

DEPTH: Same level as in pot.

HARVEST TIME: Throughout the season until frost.

HOW TO GROW WINTER SAVORY: Plant winter savory in early spring after all danger of frost. It likes full sun and a well-drained soil, but soil should be slightly sandy and reasonably moist. Each spring, cut back foliage to around two inches high.

Gardener's Tip 1
Plant will age and growth will slow down after a few years, so a new plant should be installed every four to five years.

PESTS:

There are none.

VARIETY:

Simply winter savory.

Cooking Tip 1
Although winter savory is very similar to summer savory in peppery taste, the leaves of winter savory are somewhat coarser and the flavor more intense. For this reason, Summer savory is used more in cooking than the winter variety.

SESAME SEED

(Sesamum indicum)

Sesame seed is the oldest known oil-producing seed grown by man. Its cultivation is recorded in China in 3000 BC, and the Egyptians grew it before Moses's time. There has always been a mysterious aura surrounding the seed, and yes, the magic words "Open sesame," uttered by *Ali Baba in Ali Baba and the Forty Thieves* refer to this seed. You can grow it easily in your own garden.

HARDINESS: Annual, tender.

WHEN TO PLANT: After all danger of frost, from mid-may to early June.

SPACING: Plant 1 inch apart and thin to 6 inches apart when seedlings are 2 inches high.

DEPTH: 1/4 inch.

HARVEST TIME: In the fall when flowers have dried, but before seed pods burst.

HOW TO GROW SESAME SEED: Wait until the soil warms thoroughly and plant the seed 1 inch apart, 1/4 inch deep, in full sun. This to 6 inches apart when seedlings are 2 inches high. As the plant grows it will reach a height from 2 to 9 feet, depending on growing conditions. One to three flowers will grow on the leaf axils from pods which are gathered for the crop. Keep weeded and watered during the summer. When flowers have dried, pick them off and harvest the seeds. Store in airtight containers in a cool, dry, dark place.

GARDENER'S TIP 1

For best results, plant your seeds along a south wall, as sesame needs long hot days of sun and warm nights. Do not attempt to grow this plant in the far northern reaches of the country.

GARDENER'S TIP 2

The late Mr. Philip Haralambou, who was a native of Cyprus and a friend and neighbor, told me that in Cyprus, people harvest the flowers just before they are completely dry and then place them on a sheet in the sun to dry. You would do well to follow his advice, as when sesame pods are ripe, they pop open and scatter the seeds.

PESTS: There are none.

VARIETY: Sesame.

COOKING TIP 1

Once you've developed an addiction to sesame seeds, like garlic, you'll find an excuse to add them to almost anything. However, you've probably never thought of adding them to creamed spinach or Swiss chard. It's a simple trick, but the nutty flavor added to the vegetable is terrific.

SWEET BAY

(Laurel nobilis)

Sweet Bay is a popular plant in the southern part of the United States. It is a shrub, which is easily grown. It is the laurel of ancient history, cultivated for centuries by the Greeks and Romans. The Laurel wreath, an ancient symbol of victory, is made of the leaves of this plant. It is often trained as topiary or sheared into various tree shapes for special display. In early June, the plant sports greenish white flowers, which are not all that attractive. When used as a decorative plant, it is grown primarily for its foliage.

HARDINESS: Perennial, hardy to Zone 7.

WHEN TO PLANT: In spring after all danger of frost or in late fall, before ground freezes.

SPACING: Use as specimen tree and allow plenty of space as mature plants grow to 30 feet.

DEPTH: At level of plant in container.

HARVEST TIME: Pick leaves all during the season for culinary purposes.

HOW TO GROW SWEET BAY: Sweet Bay prefers full sun, but will thrive in semi-shade. Although it is drought resistant, better results are secured if the plant is kept evenly moist during the dry summer months. An average soil is suitable, but add some rotted compost or peat moss to the soil when you install the plant. To keep it in bounds, shear the plant regularly.

GARDENER'S TIP 1

It is best to order this plant from a nursery or mail order source. Growing from cuttings and seeds is difficult and should be left to professionals. To keep plant in bounds, shear it regularly.

PESTS: Bay has a tendency to develop scale. Try to catch it early and treat by rubbing away the scale with cotton-tipped swaps dipped in rubbing alcohol. Bay grown outdoors is less likely to be invaded. White fly can also be a problem.

VARIETIES: Simply Sweet Bay.

COOKING TIP 1

The leaves of Sweet Bay are none other than the bay leaves which are used to flavor so many different foods.

SWEET WOODRUFF

(Galium odoratum)

Here's an herb which is used to make the traditional May wine of Germany. However, beyond its culinary use, Sweet Woodruff is very utilitarian in the landscape as a ground cover. Growing to about 4 inches, it sports lavish glossy green foliage and white flowers in spring.

HARDINESS: Perennial, hardy.

WHEN TO PLANT: In early spring after all danger of frost, throughout the season and until a hard frost in the fall.

SPACING: About one foot apart.

DEPTH: At level of plant in pot.

HARVEST TIME: All during season.

HOW TO GROW SWEET WOODRUFF: Once established, Sweet Woodruff can tolerate varying growing conditions but it prefers moist, rich, slightly shady conditions. It spreads rapidly when it is happy.

GARDENER'S TIP 1

Use this plant as a ground cover. Glossy attractive green foliage and white blossoms in spring make this a very useful landscape plant.

PESTS: There are none.

VARIETIES: Simply sweet woodruff.

COOKING TIP 1

May Day has been an occasion to celebrate for many centuries. Some greet it with flowers, the French with a spray of Lily of the Valley, others with maypole dances and May baskets. The Germans celebrate with May wine. Here's the recipe. You can easily halve it if you find a gallon of wine too much to use.

1 gallon dry white wine
4 tablespoons shredded fresh sweet woodruff.
1/3 cup granulated sugar (optional)
1 bottle champagne or ginger ale
Fresh strawberries and sprigs of fresh woodruff for garnish.

1. Pour one quart dry white wine into a bowl and add 4 tablespoons of fresh shredded sweet woodruff. Let soak overnight, stirring occasionally.
2. Strain to remove all pieces of herb.
3. Stir in 1 bottle chilled champagne or ginger ale, 1/3 cup sugar (if desired) and remaining 3 quarts of white wine.
4. Mix and serve with a fresh strawberry and sprigs of fresh woodruff in each glass.

TARRAGON

(Artemisia dracunculus)

Tarragon can be somewhat difficult to grow, depending on your climate. First of all, be advised that the tarragon available in nurseries is not always the genuine French article, but may be the more robust Russian tarragon which is useless to cooks. Another problem with tarragon is that its needs in terms of soil are minimal. This works to your advantage in some situations; in many parts of the Southwest, tarragon tends to flourish effortlessly. But if you grow this herb in rich soil, it will probably die. This herb also seems to grow especially well in seacoast areas of this country. Since it is a native of the Mediterranean area, poor soil, full sun, and some moisture are required for best results. In addition, growing from seed is also difficult. Your best bet will be to order a French tarragon from a reputable nursery.

HARDINESS: Perennial, hardy.

WHEN TO PLANT: After all danger of frost, from mid-May to early June.

SPACING: Depending on growing conditions, 1 to 2 feet apart.

DEPTH: Soil line of plant.

HARVEST TIME: Throughout the season.

HOW TO GROW TARRAGON: Select a sunny spot and plant your stock at the soil level at which it grew in the nursery. Plant in poor soil, preferably rocky. Ideally this plant will grow to 2 to 3 feet tall, almost like a small shrub. Set your plants about 2 feet apart. Water during extreme dry spells. Harvest leaves throughout the season and dry some for winter use.

GARDENER'S TIP 1

To dry, pick stalks early in the morning, tie them up, and hang upside down in a cool, shady, dry place. When dry, about 2 to 3 weeks later, remove the leaves from the stalks, store in airtight containers, and place in a cool, dark, dry place.

PESTS: There are none.

VARIETY: Usually there are two available: French and Russian. Purchase only from a reputable dealer and insist on French Tarragon. Russian grows in a rangy manner and the taste of the leaves is strong and overpowering. The French version is the genuine article.

COOKING TIP 1

To make tarragon vinegar, simply place about six sprigs of tarragon leaves in a pint jar of white vinegar. Cover and allow to steep for several months. Use as needed. Once steeped, do not remove the leaves from the jar. Tarragon vinegar will keep indefinitely.

THYME

(Thymus)

Thyme is a staple in all cooking, both gourmet domestic and gourmet foreign. The home-grown fresh variety is infinitely superior to commercial versions. Like mints, thyme is available in a variety of flavors, as well as in different growth habits.

HARDINESS: Perennial, hardy.

WHEN TO PLANT: From early spring through midsummer.

SPACING: Set plants about 2 feet apart.

DEPTH: Plant at soil line on stock.

HARVEST TIME: Throughout the season when needed and into fall for drying.

VARIETIES:

Creeping Caraway-Scented Thyme: If caraway seeds get stuck in your teeth or dentures, this variety should appeal to you.

Creeping Red Thyme: A dwarf creeping variety covered with purplish red flowers. It is strongly scented.

Creeping White Moss Thyme: Emerald green, a mat-like grower with tiny white flowers. This is mildly scented.

English Thyme: The common thyme commercially grown and good for cooking.

French Thyme: That preferred by French chefs. The flavor is considerably more subtle and the leaves are narrow and daintier than those of English Thyme.

Lemon Thyme: A superb thyme for cooking, especially good with chicken and with lentils. Lemon-scented leaves make good herbal tea.

HOW TO GROW THYME: Plant your stock in a sunny spot. Any type of soil will suffice. Thyme is native to the Mediterranean area where sun shines, rain doesn't fall, and soil is poor. Once established, the plants are virtually indestructible and will grow more beautiful with each passing year.

GARDENER'S TIP 1

For a poetic experience, plant the creeping varieties, Creeping Red and Creeping White Moss, between bricks or flagstones on your patio or in garden paths. As you walk over the plants and bruise them, the scent of thyme will fill the air.

GARDENER'S TIP 2

To dry for winter, cut the stalks before they flower, wash to remove dirt and insects, tie them together, and hang them upside down in a cool, dry, shady place. When they have dried, after several weeks, remove the leaves and store in airtight containers in a cool, dry place until ready to use. Your herbs will have a more pungent taste if you grind the leaves to a powdery consistency as you use them.

GARDENER'S TIP 3

Be sure not to overwater thyme. If you do, it will die.

PESTS: There are none.

VARIETIES: All of the above.

COOKING TIP 1

Use thyme in chowders, teas, salads. This herb is also an excellent complement to green beans.

COOKING TIP 2

Lemon thyme is especially good in chicken broth, soups and with lentil dishes.

EDIBLE FLOWERS

Of late, for aesthetic as well as culinary pleasure, edible flowers have become an interesting aspect of contemporary cuisine. But this is nothing new. Flowers have been enjoyed as food since ancient history and many are closely associated with certain cultures. Daylily buds have been commonly used in oriental dishes. The Romans used mallow, rose and violet in their cuisine. Italians, Spanish and Greeks use squash blossoms in their cooking. Victorians the world over were fond of rose petals and rose hips, which persist in popularity to this day: in jelly, in the bath, in teas, in desserts. In India, Greece, Cyprus, throughout the Middle East, rosewater is often an essential ingredient in elegant desserts.

Here are just a few uses for edible flowers. Use them fresh in salads, as garnish dishes, adding color and taste to salad vinaigrettes, making festive ice rings, and as candied flowers. For candied flowers, petals are brushed with egg white mixed with a little water and sprinkled with granulated sugar and then allowed to dry.

Below is a list of tasty and very edible flowers. When collecting flowers to use as food, be sure you have identified your flowers correctly. Some grocery stores now offer edible flowers in their produce section along with fresh herbs and salad greens.

When collecting, select flowers that are freshly opened and free of insect and disease damage. Caution: If you are going to eat your flowers, it is best not to use pesticides, despite what you may be told by garden centers, nurseries or even "experts."Although many pesticides have been approved for controlling pests on flowers which may later be consumed, it is not a good idea. Avoid using commercially grown cut flowers as they are often heavily treated with pesticides.

COOKING TIP 1

When you add flowers to food, experiment. Start out with small amounts so that the food will not be overpowered by the taste and smell of the flowers. Also flowers are usually a nice addition to a dish and should be used for color, subtle flavor and taste.

COOKING TIP 1

Stamens and styles found in flowers' centers may cause an allergic reaction. To be on the safe side, remove them before eating.

COOKING TIP 2

Here's a simple recipe for making candied flower blossoms. You will need whisked egg whites. With fingers, gently dab mixture evenly on both sides of flowers. (Don't dip flowers or coating will be too thick.) Sprinkle superfine granulated sugar over both sides of flowers until evenly coated. Place on a wire rack to dry, at least 8 hours.

Here is a list of flowers which can be eaten.

Anise hyssop
Arugula
Bachelor Buttons
Basil
Bee Balm
Borage
Begonia
Burnet
Broccoli
Calendula
Carnations
Chamomile
Chicory (bitter)
Chives
Chrysanthemum (bitter)
Cilantro
Clover
Coriander
Chervil
Cucumber
Daisy
Dandelion
Daylily
Dewberry
Dianthus
Dill
Elderberry
English Daisy
Fennel
Gladiolus
Garlic chives
Geraniums
Ginger
Hibiscus
Hollyhock

Honeysuckle
Jasmine
Johnny Jump up
Lovage
Lavender
Lilac
Marigold
Marjoram
Mint
Mustard
Nasturtium
Okra
Orange
Oregano
Pansy
Parsley
Pea
Radish
Redbud
Rose
Rosemary
Runner bean
Safflower
Sage
Savory
Scarlet
Scented Geranium
Snapdragon
Society garlic
Squash
Thyme
Tulip
Violet
Wood sorrel
Yucca
Zucchini

BERRIES

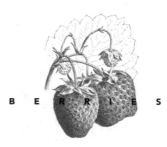

T HERE ARE THREE GOOD REASONS for growing your own berries. First, fresh home-grown berries are always superior in taste and quality to anything you can purchase in the markets. Second, more often than not, most varieties of berries are simply not available unless you grow them yourself. The reason for this is they are very perishable and do not ship well. And third, if they are available, they are usually outrageously expensive.

Just think of having more raspberries at your disposal than you can use! This luxury can be yours with a minimum investment of time, money, and space.

BLACKBERRIES

(Rubus)

Fresh blackberries are rarely available in the markets. So, if you enjoy these delicious morsels you must grow your own in your garden. There is nothing complicated about growing blackberries, but keep your patch contained, as blackberries have a tendency to spread.

HARDINESS: Hardy perennial.

WHEN TO PLANT: In spring, when the ground is workable.

SPACING: In rows 7 to 8 feet apart, with plants about 3 to 5 feet apart.

DEPTH: Soil line of stock.

HARVEST TIME: In early and midsummer when berries are ripe.

HOW TO GROW BLACKBERRIES: Order your stock from a mail order nursery, as few local garden centers stock this variety of berry. There are two types of blackberries: those which trail and those which grow erect. The trailing types are not fully hardy in the most northerly states and need support when they grow. If you do not provide this, your patch will become an ugly, unmanageable mess. Unless you are prepared for this extra work, and have lots of space, you would do well to purchase only the erect varieties. This variety develops arched canes which are self-supporting.

Blackberries are not fussy about soil as long as moisture is abundant. Ideally, sand loam with a good supply of humus worked in is most to their liking. Keep in mind when locating your patch that you will need access to a supply of water, as blackberries need a lot of moisture during the period when the berries are developing.

Prepare the soil by adding several bushels of rotted manure for each 50-foot row. Or, if you wish, you can work in 3 to 4 pounds of 5-10-5 fertilizer or organic mixture. Cultivate to keep weeds free, and water copiously during berry set and hot summer months.

How to thin Blackberry Canes

The new canes which grow from your plants will live for only 2 years, so they must be cut out at the end of each season. Keep in mind that the new canes produce side shoots the first year, and during the second year, these side shoots throw blossoms which ripen into fruit. Once the cane has fruited, it dies.

How to prune Blackberries

A certain amount of pruning is necessary if you want a bumper harvest of large berries. In the fall of the first year, the new stalks will have sent out side branches. These are called laterals. Cut these back from four to six buds on each lateral.

WHEN TO HARVEST: Blackberries ripen in early to midsummer. When they are ready to eat, they will be firm and sweet. Do not let them get soft and overripe.

GARDENER'S TIP 1

In colder regions, you will have to protect your creeping plants. At the end of the season untie, bend over the canes to the ground, and cover them with a layer of earth, compost, or hay. Then in the spring, when the weather warms up, uncover them.

PESTS: Blackberries are reasonably resistant to insect invasions. Keep your patch clean by removing old canes and any patches of wild raspberries or wild blackberries which might be nearby. Diseases often start in the wild patches and then move on to your more sophisticated plants.

VARIETIES: Darrow and Thornfree (this is less prolific but has the advantage of having no thorns).

COOKING TIP 1

A favorite of mine is cold blackberry soup. Wash and pick over 1 pound of ripe blackberries. Put in a saucepan with 1 lemon, thinly sliced, 2 cups cold water, a 1-inch stick of cinnamon, 2 cloves, and 1/2 cup granulated sugar. Bring to a boil, lower the flame, and simmer gently for 10 minutes or until the fruit is soft. Rub through a fine sieve and chill well. Just before serving, stir in 2 cups chilled sour cream. You can also use wild blackberries to make this soup.

BLUEBERRIES

(Vaccinium)

Although blueberries are usually available in the market, they are such handsome and hardy plants that you should consider growing them in your garden. If you select a range of varieties from early to late bearing, you will have a continuous supply of these delicious berries all summer.

HARDINESS: Shrubby perennial, hardy.

WHEN TO PLANT: In early spring, while dormant.

SPACING: 3 to 8 feet apart, in rows 5 to 8 feet apart.

DEPTH: At soil level of stock.

HARVEST TIME: From early summer to late summer, depending on variety.

HOW TO GROW BLUEBERRIES: Perhaps the most important thing you must keep in mind when planting your blueberry bushes is that these berries require an acid soil. If you do not know whether or not the soil in your area is acidic, inquire of neighbors or local nursery people. Beyond that, you can always purchase an inexpensive soil testing kit to determine whether or not you will have to take steps to correct the acidic composition of your planting area. A pH of 4.0 to 4.8 is best, although some people have luck with these plants when the pH is as high as 5.0. If your pH is higher than that, you may have to add sulfate of ammonia to your soil regularly in order to maintain the proper acidity. If you find that azalea and rhododendron thrive in your garden, blueberries probably will as well.

To help your plants get a good start, dig deep holes and mix in a considerable amount of peat moss, rotted manure, and compost. At the same time, once you have determined the pH of your soil, add sulfate of ammonia as indicated by a soil test.

You can purchase your blueberry plants from a local nursery. However, the range of varieties will probably be limited. Keep in mind that it is advisable to plant two or more different varieties in order to secure maximum cross-pollination. A good idea is to select stock from early, midseason, and late-bearing varieties. Order from a reliable mail order house, as they almost always have a reasonable selection. But be sure to order early, as generally supplies are limited. If possible, order two- or three-year-old plants.

When your plants arrive, plant them at the level at which they grew in the nursery. Water thoroughly and mulch the soil around the plants with 3 or 4 inches of acidic peat moss, sawdust, or wood chips. Remove all fruit buds the first year, so that the plants' energy will be directed to root growth.

During droughts water at least 1 inch a week and keep weeds at a minimum by cultivating. Do not cultivate too deeply or you will disturb surface roots.

HOW TO PRUNE BLUEBERRY BUSHES For larger berries, although smaller yield, prune your bushes lightly. Remove the small, slender branches and leave the strong vigorous shoots. These will always produce the largest berries. Prune in early spring when plant is still dormant. As the bush grows, be sure to "open it up," that is, remove some of the inner branches so that air circulation and sunlight are permitted to aid your plants in their productivity.

Gardener's Tip 1

A full-grown blueberry bush should produce from 8 to 10 quarts of berries per year.

Gardener's Tip 2

You must net these bushes to protect the fruit from the birds.

Gardener's Tip 3

Blueberries are handsome plants and can be incorporated into your landscape design. In May, pinkish white flowers appear, followed by fruit, and in the fall the leaves turn red. In winter the red and green twigs and red buds are attractive.

PESTS: There are none, except birds.

VARIETIES: In order of ripening: Earliblue, Blueray, Atlantic, Jersey, Burlington, Coville.

Cooking Tip 1

A blueberry pie with uncooked fresh berries is much more to my taste than one using cooked or baked berries. Here's a recipe that I use. You can do the same thing with fresh peaches, strawberries, or any other very fresh and ripe fruit or berry. Use your favorite pie crust recipe and make a 9-inch pie crust. Be sure to prick the bottom of the crust with a fork. Bake and set aside. In a 2-quart pot put 1-1/3 cups sugar and 1/2 cup water. Bring to a boil and reduce heat. Then dissolve 1/4 cup cornstarch in 3/4 cup water. Add to sugar water and cook about 10 minutes, stirring constantly, until the mixture is clear. Cool and add 1 tablespoon lemon juice and 1/8 teaspoon salt. Add to fresh fruit or berries and mix gently. When mixture is completely cool, place in baked pie crust. Serve with whipped cream.

If you use fresh peaches or strawberries for this pie, reduce sugar to 3/4 cup and water to 1/4 cup. Dissolve cornstarch in 1/2 cup water. Add vanilla or almond extract to the fresh peaches if you make a peach pie.

RED CURRANTS

(Ribes)

Where would a discriminating cook be without currant jelly to use as a glaze on meats, poultry, and pastry? Currants are easily grown, are not fussy about soil, and will thrive in semishade or sun. This coupled with the fact that the bushes are attractive—coordinate them in your landscape scheme. And, when the currant bushes are in flower, prepare for a sensuous moment: Currant flowers have a delightful perfume, delicate and permeating at the same time, and completely irresistable to bees.

HARDINESS: Shrubby perennial, hardy.

WHEN TO PLANT: Early spring before dormancy is broken.

SPACING: About 5 feet apart.

DEPTH: At soil line of stock.

HARVEST TIME: Early to midseason, depending on variety.

HOW TO GROW CURRANTS: Order your plants from a reliable mail order house or purchase them at your local nursery. Keep in mind that most local nurseries do not stock this plant, so if you wish to include them in your garden, inquire early so that you can order by mail if necessary. Currants grow readily in most soils, from clay loam to heavy clay. The one kind of soil they do not like is sandy soil. If that is your soil condition, plant your bushes in a well-shaded spot, even on the north side of your house.

Dig a good-size hole, spread the roots out over a cone of earth, and fill with soil. Water thoroughly.

Mulch your bushes heavily. This will help keep the soil cool, retain moisture, and eliminate the need for cultivation which might damage the surface roots. In addition, the mulch will provide nutrients for the soil as it decomposes.

Each spring, before you apply the mulch, put about 1 inch of compost or rotted manure on the surface of the soil. Water during droughts.

Currants bear on year-old wood and at the bottom of older wood, so you must prune your bushes each fall after the plants go dormant. The recommended practice is to prune out all three-year-old wood. You can also pinch back new growth in late spring in order to foster leaf cover and new growth.

Gardener's Tip 1

Propagating currants is easy. In the fall, after the leaves begin to drop, cut wood from strong, healthy plants. Select the thickest branches. Cut the tops straight across and the bottoms at any angle. In this way, you'll be able to tell which end is the top and which end is the bottom. The cuttings should be about 10 to 12 inches long. Tie the cuttings in a bundle, dig a pit, place the cuttings at the bottom, and cover them. In the spring, dig them up and plant them, bottom end down. They will have healthy roots on them by that time.

Gardener's Tip 2

Birds relish currants, so if you want any left for yourself, you will have to net your entire stand of bushes. Be sure to follow this advice. If you don't, you will not have one single berry left on your bushes.

PESTS: Currants are pest-free, except for birds.

VARIETIES: Cherry, an early variety; Diploma, which has the reputation of being best for jelly and syrup; Perfection, for good table eating; and Red Lake, a midseason variety.

Cooking Tip 1

To make an excellent syrup follow these instructions: Place 4 quarts of berries in a gallon jug. (This recipe can be used to make raspberry or strawberry syrup as well.) Let stand in the sun for 4 days. Be sure to cover the jar with about five or six layers of cheesecloth. Extract the juice from the berries by squeezing them in the jar. Strain and place in a saucepan with 4 cups sugar. Cook about 6 minutes or just to the boiling point. Pour into hot sterilized jars and process. If a few fruit flies should find their way through the cheesecloth into the juice, merely pick or strain them out. They are harmless.

ELDERBERRIES

(Sambucus canadiensis)

Blue or black elderberries grow wild throughout much of the United States and Canada. Avoid plants which bear red elderberries because the berries are poisonous. The plant grows to about 20 feet, and at maturity is fountain-shaped.

HARDINESS: Perennial, hardy.

WHEN TO PLANT: In spring, after all danger of frost.

SPACING: At least 10 feet apart. You will need two for cross pollination. Elderberry is self-unfruitful.

DEPTH: Level at which plant grew in nursery.

HARVEST TIME: Mid to late summer, depending on location.

HOW TO GROW ELDERBERRIES: Plant in full sun or partial shade in well-drained average soil. Buy elderberries from a reputable nursery or mail order house. You will need two in order to pollinate. If you buy only one you will have no berries. Prepare ground before planting. Dig a hole about 18 inches deep by 18 inches in diameter and fortify the soil with about fifty percent well rotted compost or sphagnum peat moss. Remove the plant from container and set in ground. Water well the first year until well established.

GARDENER'S TIP 1

To keep plant in bounds remove tallest and oldest stems every year in late winter.

GARDENER'S TIP 2

Prune each year by removing stems that have borne fruit for several years to allow younger growth to mature. Use long handled loppers or a pruning saw to do the job.

PESTS: There are none.

VARIETIES: Adams ripens early August; Johns is vigorous but not as productive as other cultivars; Kent earlier than Adams; Nova large fruit is sweeter than other varieties; York, the largest berry of all. Ripens late August, early September.

COOKING TIP 1

Elderberries have been used for wine, pies and jelly for hundreds of years. For pies and jelly, use any blueberry pie or raspberry jelly recipe and substitute elderberries.

COOKING TIP 2

Flowers are edible. Dip in fritter batter and fry quickly and serve with a berry syrup. Fried flowers resemble lace and look very attractive when served as a compliment with a dessert.

FRAISES DES BOIS
(ALPINE STRAWBERRIES)

(Fragaria vesca)

Undoubtedly, if you have visited the finer restaurants of Belgium and France, you've probably seen these berries on menus and perhaps have even ordered and savored them. The flavor is so intense, and a great treat for strawberry enthusiasts, human and otherwise. Our late Basset Hound Diana, was addicted to them, and certainly consumed more than her share, eating them right off the plant.

Classically, they are served with clotted cream or creme fraiche. They are available in this country at posh good emporiums, but prices are exorbitant because they are flown over fresh from Europe. Once you've planted your stock, each year you can triple or quadruple your plants by dividing, so although the initial outlay may be more than you'd care to spend, in the long run, these plants are very inexpensive. They run about $24 a dozen. There are no tricks to growing fraises des bois—in fact, they are more easily grown than our own very delicious cultivated varieties.

HARDINESS: Perennial, hardy.

WHEN TO PLANT: In early spring, as soon as ground in workable.

SPACING: About 1 foot apart.

DEPTH: Where crown meets root system.

HARVEST TIME: All during the season as berries ripen.

HOW TO GROW FRAISES DES BOIS: Order plants from a reliable nursery and set in the ground in very early spring, as soon as the ground is workable. If plants arrive with two or three crowns per specimen, separate them into individual plants and set in ground at crown level. There are no special soil needs for fraises des bois, and they seem to thrive in either full sun or partial shade if they are kept well watered.

You can also plant fraises des bois from seed. Sow indoors from January to May. After hardening off in mid-spring, set outdoors in a permanent spot.

GARDENER'S TIP 1

These plants do not send out runners as do our domestic varieties, so you can use them quite effectively as a border for a perennial bed or for lining a walk.

GARDENER'S TIP 2

Each spring dig up your plants and divide them into individual crowns and replant. Be sure to do this very early, before the leaves have unfolded.

GARDENER'S TIP 3

Fraises des bois bear fruit all through the season, until frost and beyond.

GARDENER'S TIP 4

If you wish, you can grow many varieties of fraises des bois from seed. Most mail order houses carry this berry under the name of Alpine strawberries, but they are not the same berry as those carried by White Flower Farm.

PESTS: There are none.

VARIETIES: Alpine, yellow fruited, Alexandria, Baron Solemacher, Rugen Improved. Charles V is the French variety.

COOKING TIP 1

In France, fraises des bois are served with Coeur de la Creme made in heart-shaped containers, or with creme fraiche. A reasonable facsimile of the European product can be made at home by combining 2 cups heavy cream with 1/2 tablespoon buttermilk. Simply pour 1-1/2 cups heavy cream into a Mason jar, then add the buttermilk and the rest of the cream. Screw the lid on loosely and let sit at room temperature for 14 to 18 hours. This time can vary depending on temperature. In summer the creme fraiche can thicken in 8 hours; in winter, it may take 24 hours. When thick, tighten the lid and refrigerate. Fill a container with creme fraiche and top with the tiny berries.

GOOSEBERRIES

(Ribes)

Gooseberries are an old-fashioned berry that is rarely available in the markets. Delicious tarts, pies, and an unforgettable jam are made from them. They are virtually maintenance-free and are attractive plants that can be incorporated into your landscape design

HARDINESS: Shrubby perennial, hardy.

WHEN TO PLANT: Early spring, before dormancy is broken.

SPACING: About 4 feet apart.

DEPTH: At soil line on stock.

HARVEST TIME: Midsummer, when fruit has turned from light green to plum color.

HOW TO GROW GOOSEBERRIES: Your best bet is to order from a mail order nursery, as local garden centers rarely carry stock of this berry. Gooseberries are not fussy about soil and will grow in most earth from clay loam to heavy clay. They will tolerate semi-shade, so a northern or western exposure is satisfactory. When your plants arrive, dig a good-size hole, spread the roots out over a cone of earth, and fill with soil. Water thoroughly. Mulch your plants with several inches of compost in order to preserve moisture, keep the surface roots cool, and eliminate the need for cultivation. The mulch will add nutrients to the soil as it decomposes.

Every year or so, at the end of the season, cut out the older canes to keep your plant vigorous. You can also pinch back new growth in late spring, to force new shoots and branching. This will result in a larger crop of berries.

Gardener's Tip 1

Propagating gooseberry bushes is a simple matter. Simply bend one of the branches to the ground, cover a portion of the branch with soil, and place a brick or stone on top of it. In a year or two, roots will have formed and you can cut your new plant free from the parent and set it in the soil.

Gardener's Tip 2

If you have a problem with birds eating the berries, and I never have, simply net the plants when the fruit forms.

PESTS: Gooseberries, like currants, are subject to pine blister rust. In some areas of the United States where white pine trees grow, it is illegal to plant gooseberries. Check with your County Extension Agent as to whether or not you live in a prohibited area.

Occasionally scale or borers may attack your plant. If you spot scale, spray with dormant oil spray in early spring. If borers are present, and you can tell if you see little piles of sawdust material on or near the branches, cut off the infected branches and burn or dispose of them.

VARIETY: Pixwell.

COOKING TIP 1

Before you prepare gooseberries for eating and cooking, snip off the tiny little stems that form on the end of each berry. Beyond the classic gooseberry pies and tarts so favored on the Continent, and of course, the very special gooseberry jam, these luscious small fruits can be spiced and served with duck, chicken, or other fowl as you would a cranberry sauce.

HUCKLEBERRIES

(Gaylussacia brachycera)

Huckleberry plants are treasured by seasoned gardener's. They are native American plants, elegant, slow growing, evergreen foliage which turns a rich bronze in the fall, and they grow only to about 18 inches. And in summer, plants produce fruits which are very similar to blueberries, but smaller. They are very difficult to find in nurseries or specialty houses, probably because they are very slow growing and thus expensive to grow.

HARDINESS: Perennial, hardy.

WHEN TO PLANT: In early spring or late fall.

SPACING: 2 feet.

DEPTH: At soil line on stock.

HARVEST TIME: Early to mid summer.

HOW TO GROW HUCKLEBERRIES: Cultivation is the same as for blueberries.

GARDENER'S TIP 1

Making more plants is easy. Divide the plants in early spring before growth starts and replant divisions. You can also collect seed when the plant bears fruit, and sow them when ripe.

PESTS: There are none, except birds.

VARIETY: Only the native Gaylussacia brachycera, also called Box-huckleberry is available.

COOKING TIP 1

One of my favorite summertime activities when I was a child, was to go out into the Great Swamp in Morris County, New Jersey, with my dear grandmother and pick huckleberries. Grandma made the finest huckleberry pie on earth, with her famous pie crust, which contained vinegar as one of its ingredients. Huckleberries can be used as you would use blueberries. Grandma died in 1962, and I still have two quart jars of her jarred huckleberries in the basement. They sit there as a reminder of that wonderful lady. I'm afraid to open them because they most certainly must have spoiled by now, but I just can't bring myself to throw them away. So, they just get older and older and older. Maybe next year.

RED RASPBERRIES

Red (Rubus)

The reasons why red raspberries are so outrageously expensive in the markets are twofold. First, they must be picked by hand, which means high labor costs. Second, the berries are very perishable and must be shipped to market almost immediately after picking in order to reach customers in an edible state. In fact, even with modern refrigeration, the time from picking to table probably shouldn't be any longer than 2 days. There is nothing difficult about raising your own raspberries. Once established, a bed will provide enough for your table, preserving, and other delectable treats.

HARDINESS: Hardy, but sensitive to cold in far northern areas.

WHEN TO PLANT: Early spring, as soon as ground is workable.

SPACING: In rows 5 to 8 feet apart, plants 2 to 3 feet apart.

DEPTH: Slightly below soil line on stock.

HARVEST TIME: In early summer and again in the fall if you select ever-bearing varieties.

HOW TO GROW RED RASPBERRIES: A rich, friable soil is a prerequisite for growing red raspberries, so if your soil is not up to par, fortify it with generous amounts of rotted manure, compost, and peat moss. The reason is that these delectable berries need plenty of moisture to develop properly and the improved soil will retain the moisture better. Plan on at least a bushel of organic fortification for every six plants.

Once you've established ideal soil conditions, purchase your plants. You have two alternatives. Either order them by mail from reliable seed houses or buy them at your local garden center. But, and most important, buy only virus-free healthy plants. There are two distinct kinds of raspberries: those that bear part of their crop in the fall and the balance in late spring or early summer and those that bear in July on the previous year's growth. The first kind are called "ever-bearing" and I recommend them highly.

After your plants have arrived, get them into the ground as soon as possible. If the roots are a little dry, soak them in a pail of water for an hour or two before planting. Red raspberries should be set into the ground about 1 inch below nursery level. Plant them 2 to 3 feet apart, in rows from 5 to 8 feet apart. Cultivate to remove weeds, but be careful not to injure the new shoots or surface roots. Provide plenty of water during the first season of growth.

HOW TO PRUNE RED RASPBERRIES: After planting, there is a moderate amount of yearly maintenance involved in the cultivation of raspberries. First keep in mind that the ever-bearing varieties will produce two crops a year: one in the fall and one in June or July. The July crop bears on last year's growth in both kinds of berries. Once it has produced a crop, the canes die. In the meantime, at the base of each plant the new canes which will produce the fall crop in the case of "ever-bearers" and the subsequent July crop will begin to grow. This means that each year the old canes must be removed. You can do this either after you have picked the July crop or in late fall, when the plants go into dormancy. I have found it an easier task to remove the spent and now dead canes in the fall. You will have no difficulty in distinguishing between the old canes and the new September canes.

Beyond that, each fall, head back the canes by cutting them back to 3 feet. Cut them back to 36 inches. In this way, each plant will branch in the spring and produce a more abundant crop.

GARDENER'S TIP 1

Raspberries ripen rapidly at harvest time. When your berries are bright red and part easily from the stem, it is time to pick. Daily picking is necessary, as these perishable berries deteriorate on the canes once ripe. Excess berries may be frozen readily. Simply place the berries in airtight containers and put them in the freezer. Use these later to make jelly, jam, or syrup.

GARDENER'S TIP 2

Keep your raspberry patch contained. You will notice new shoots emerging from the ground as far away as 6 to 8 feet from your patch. Dig them out, then plant them elsewhere, give them to friends or neighbors, or dispose of them.

GARDENER'S TIP 3

When you install your raspberries, be absolutely certain you have access to both sides of each row. This will facilitate maintenance and harvesting. I plant mine in a single row. Do not plant your patch along a fence, wall, or shrub border, if you can help it.

PESTS: Virus diseases pose the greatest problems, and prevention is the best cure. Be sure to purchase plants only from reliable nurseries or mail order houses. Keep the patch weed-free, and cut out all old or diseased canes. If a virus problem emerges, the only solution is to start a new bed, choosing a different section of your garden for it, or if this is impossible, wait several years before replanting.

Occasionally raspberry crown borer may strike. These are white, grub-like larvae which burrow into bark at the plant's base. A 25 percent Diazinon EC solution should be used to drench crowns and lower canes around the latter part of the growing season. Repeat this again 2 weeks later. Do not use this chemical if fruit is on the plant.

VARIETY: Ever-bearing: Heritage (red). Standard (bears once a season, in early summer: Nova (red), Taylor (red). OR TRY YELLOW OR BLACK RASPBERRIES: Ever-bearing: Goldie (Yellow), Standard: Fallgold (yellow); Black Treasure (black); Allen (black), Cumberland (black).

COOKING TIP 1

After your bed is established, you will have a bumper crop. Here are some ideas as to what to do with the surfeit. Try making raspberry jelly instead of jam. There are no pits to make the taste bitter. Follow instructions for syrup included in section on currants. But here is a triumph you might want to try: In the past few years, vinaigre de framboise (raspberry vinegar) has become very popular with sophisticated cooks. The only problem is that it costs anywhere from $10 to $15 a pint in specialty stores. You can make it at home for the cost of a bottle of white vinegar if you have a supply of fresh raspberries.

Simply fill a 2-quart jar with fresh raspberries and then pour in enough white vinegar to cover. Cover the top of the jar with about five thicknesses of cheesecloth and tie securely or fasten with a rubber band.

Place the jar in a sunny window for about 4 to 5 weeks. At the end of that time, the berries will have turned white and the vinegar a deep wine red. Remove the cheesecloth and strain the mixture first through a kitchen sieve, and then through several layers of cheesecloth. If any fruit flies find their way through the cheesecloth covering during the brewing stage, just pick them out. Bottle the vinegar, cover, and place in the refrigerator. It will keep indefinitely.

COOKING TIP 2

Now what do you do with raspberry vinegar? First you can use it in dressings for shellfish salads in place of white wine or cider vinegar. It imparts a delicate, fruity taste to the salad.

My favorite use for this ruby delight is to make a sauce for liver, kidney, or other organ meats. Here's an easy recipe: Sauté calve's liver (or for that matter, deveined beef liver) in butter. When it is nicely browned, but still pink inside, remove it from the frying pan and keep warm in the oven. Then pour about 1/3 cup raspberry vinegar into the frying pan and mix it with the browned butter and pan juices. As you bring it to a boil you'll notice the heady, piquant aroma. Reduce it very slightly, pour over the meat and serve. You won't believe how utterly delicious plain old liver tastes when prepared in this manner. You can also fix veal kidneys in the same way. Once you've tasted both of these, you'll find yourself experimenting to find other uses for this treat.

SOURCES

S E E D S   A N D   P L A N T   S T O C K ,
G A R D E N I N G   S U P P L I E S

The Cook's Garden
PO Box 535
Londonderry, VT 05148
800-457-9703
FAX:
800-457-9705
WEB SITE:
http://www.cooksgarden.com
Wide variety of unusual vegetable
seeds, including many French and
Italian varieties.

Geo. W. Park Seed Co. Inc.
1 Parkton Ave.
Greenwood, SC 29647-0001
800-845-3369
FAX: **800-275-9941**
Email: **info@parkseed.com**
WEB SITE: **www.parkseed.com**
The old standby, offering many heir-
loom vegetable and flower seeds.

Johnny's Seeds
1 Foss Hill Road
RR 1, Box 2580
Albion, ME 04910-9731
207-437-4395
FAX: **800-437-4395**
WEB SITE:
http://www.johnnyseeds.com
Many foreign vegetable cultivar and
heirloom varieties.

Kitazawa Seed Co.
1111 Chapman St.
San Jose, CA 95126-1104
408-243-1330
One of the few sources for Oriental
vegetable seeds.

Ronnigers Seed and Potato Co.
PO Box 307
Ellensburg, WA 98926
800-846-6178
The most comprehensive selection of
potatoes available in the US. Also
rhubarb, garlic, shallots, asparagus,
sweet potatoes and onion sets.

Seeds of Change
Box 15700
Santa Fe, NM 87506-5700
800-957-3337
Source for garlic varieties.

Seeds of Distinction
PO Box 86, Station A
Etobicoke (Toronto), ON
CANADA, M9C 4V2
416-255-3060
FAX: **888-327-9193**
WEBSITE:
www.SEEDSofDISTINCTION.com
E-MAIL:
seeds@SEEDSofDISTINCTION.COM

Shepherd's Garden Seeds
30 Irene St.
Torrington, CT 06790
860-482-3638
FAX: 860-482-0532
WEB SITE:
http://www.shepherdseeds.com
Many unusual offerings for the
gourmet gardener.

Southern Exposure Seed Exchange
Box 170
Earlysville, VA 22936
804-973-4703
Source for various garlics.

Thompson & Morgan, Inc.
PO Box 1308
Jackson, NJ 08527-0308
800-274-7333
FAX: 888-466-4769
An impressive and remarkably com-
prehensive collection of vegetable and
flower seeds.

W. Atlee Burpee & Co.
300 Park Avenue
Warminster, PA 189974
800-888-1447
FAX: 800-487-5530
WEB SITE: www.burpee.com
The old standby, now offering heir-
loom seeds.

White Flower Farm
PO Box 50
Litchfield, CT 06759-0050
800-503-9624
FAX: 860-411-6159
WEB SITE: http://www.whiteflower-
farm.com
As always, the best source for Alpine
Strawberries (Fraise des Bois) and the
purveyor of numerous other great
plants.

R. H. Shumway
Box 1
Graniteville, SC 29829-0001
803-663-9771
FAX: 888-437-2733
Shumway's catalogue is a delight for
its period engravings of vegetables and
flowers as well as for its fine selection
of edible plants.

Totally Tomatoes
Box 1626
Augusta, GA 30903-1626
803-663-0016
FAX: 888-477-7333
One glance at their catalogue will
prove that Totally Tomatoes is, indeed,
"devoted to the avid tomato grower."
You won't believe the range of choices,
but they sell only seed so be prepared
to start your own plants.

Logee's Greenhouses
141 North Street
Danielson, CT 06239
860-774-8030
FAX: 860-774-9932
105 years in the business, Logee's does
not specialize in edible plants, but has
the indisputable claim to the widest
array of rare plants and an excellent
collection of herb plants.

Weiss Brothers' Nursery
11690 Colfax Highway
Grass Valley, CA 95945
530-272-7657
FAX: 503-272-3578
Weiss deals only in perennials, and
carries a fine selection of herbs and
flowers.

Henry Fields Seed and Nursery Co.
415 North Burnett
Shenandoah, Iowa 51602
605-665-4491
FAX: 503-665-2601
Large variety of vegetables, herbs, and
berries, plus flowers and supplies.

Gurney's Seed and Nursery Co.
110 Capital Street
Yankton, South Dakota 57079
605-665-1930
FAX: 605-665-9718
Berries, vegetables, bulbs, ground cov-
ers, plus seed starting helpers.

Mellingers, Inc.
2310 W. South Range Road
North Lima, Ohio 44452
330-549-9861
toll-free for credit card orders:
800-321-7444
FAX: 330-549-3716
Large variety of seeds and plants, plus
extensive selection of basic gardening
supplies.

Otis S. Twilley Seed Company, Inc.
P. O. Box 65
Trevose, PA 19053-0065
800-622-7333
FAX: 215-245-1949
Specialty supplier to roadside, U-Pick,
and bedding plant growers with an
extensive line of vegetables.

Seeds West Garden Seeds
P. O. Box 2817
Tao, New Mexico 87571
505-758-7268
Fine heirlooms, hybrids, and rare seeds
for western gardens. A very interesting catalogue, with an especially
extensive list of hard-to-find lettuces
and greens.

Gardens Alive!
5100 Schenley Place
Lawrenceburg, IN 47025
812-537-8650
FAX: 812-537-5108
Environmentally responsible products
from bird houses to beneficial insects.

Smith and Hawken
Two Arbor Lane, Box 6900
Florence, KY 41022-6900
800-776-3336
WEB SITE: http://www.smith-hawken.com
Upscale gardening specialties, including garden furniture, outdoor lighting, trellises, fountains.

Periodicals

Taunton's Kitchen Garden
The Taunton Press, Inc.
Newton, CT 06470-5506
203-426-8171
An excellent source of information for the avid kitchen gardener, published six times yearly, with well written articles and beautiful full color photos. Inspiration! $24 for a one-year subscription.
Taunton's also publishes a valuable periodical called **Fine Gardening.**

Garden Design
100 Avenue of the Americas
New York, NY 10013
800-234-5118
FAX: 212-334-1260
Though not devoted specifically to kitchen gardens, this magazine frequently features articles and advice on edible plants. Gorgeous and well edited, it is a fine source of ideas. From a newsstand or by subscription for $27.95 per year. From the same folks who publish the fine food magazine **Saveur.**

A

B

M

N